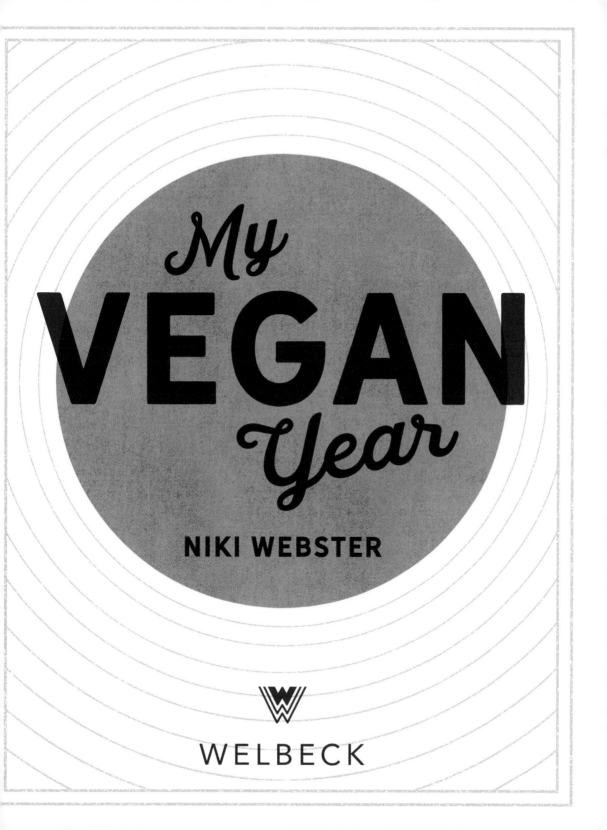

My VEGAN Year

NIKI WEBSTER

WELBECK

THANK YOU TO MY SISTER **EMS** - WHO GAVE ME A HOME AND MOSTLY ATE MY DESSERTS.

MY LOVELY NIECES **FREYA AND TILLY** FOR TASTE TESTING AND BEING EVER HONEST.

THANK YOU TO **CRAIG** FOR THE INVALUABLE GROWING KNOWLEDGE AND SUSTAINING WALKS DURING THIS TESTING TIME.

AND ALL MY **WONDERFUL FRIENDS AND FAMILY** FOR THEIR HELP, ADVICE, AND ONGOING AND HUGELY APPRECIATED SUPPORT.

FINALLY TO **MALIN** FOR EVERYTHING X
- NIKI

Published in 2021 by Welbeck Children's Limited part of Welbeck Publishing Group
20 Mortimer Street, London W1T 3JW, UK

Text copyright © 2021 by Nicola Webster

Nicola Webster has asserted her moral right to be identified as the Author of this Work in accordance with the Copyright Designs and Patents Act 1988.

Photograph on p7 © Sara Kiyo Popowa
All other photographs © 2020 Niki Webster
Chapter artwork © 2021 Anna Stiles

ISBN 978 1 78312 737 5

Printed in Dongguan, China

FSC
www.fsc.org
MIX
Paper from responsible sources
FSC® C144853

10 9 8 7 6 5 4 3 2 1

Author, photographer and food stylist: Niki Webster
Nutritional consultant: Jessica English, Registered Dietitian
Design Manager: Margaret Hope
Designer: Natalie Schmidt
Editor: Joff Brown
Production: Melanie Robertson

Contents

About NIKI

Hi, my name is Niki and I'm a plant-based cook and cookbook author. From a really young age I pretty much refused to eat meat! I didn't like the taste at all, and the thought of eating animals just felt wrong to me.

This was definitely a challenge for my poor mom who was left not knowing what to do, especially when I developed a milk intolerance when I was seven. Of course, back then there weren't the vegan options available like there are today. I ended up eating quite a limited diet, but this all changed when I got in the kitchen and started creating and experimenting with food.

It's been a long journey from then to now. I discovered the joy of eating and creating amazing plant-based food—all focused on natural whole foods using seasonal ingredients.

So I'm happy to have created a handbook for young people specifically focused on vegan eating throughout the whole year. I've filled it with helpful advice and inspiration about how to cut down on (or cut out) meat and dairy, as well as the latest nutritional information.

Starting in spring, you'll learn how to make amazing vegan food for every season. I've included seasonal tips, from how to grow your own veggies to how to make the ultimate vegan food for the party season.

I hope you love this plant-based companion for 365 days of being vegan!

Niki x

Being Vegan through the YEAR

If you are considering becoming vegan or trying a vegan lifestyle, your reasons may be varied: it could be animal welfare, helping the environment, for health reasons, or a combination of all of them.

But what does it actually mean to be vegan? Veganism is a lifestyle that doesn't use anything from animals—so that means no meat, fish, and dairy. It also means avoiding anything made from animals like clothes, cosmetics, and household items. This can be challenging, especially when you are starting your vegan journey.

DON'T MISS OUT

Even though there are some amazing plant-based options out there, it can still be hard at times... for example, during birthdays and celebrations when you are with family and friends who may not be vegan. The good news is you don't need to miss out at all—you can make impressive celebration food like cakes and snacks which you'd never know were vegan at all and you and your guests will love!

EATING SEASONALLY AND LOCALLY

The next thing you might want to do is make steps toward eating seasonally and locally. There are many benefits—it's usually fresher, it's better for the environment as it means fewer food miles, you can support local businesses, and it lets you get creative with seasonal produce.

> "Veganism is a lifestyle that doesn't use anything from animals"

GROWING YOUR OWN FRUIT, VEGETABLES, AND HERBS

It might be easy and convenient to buy produce from the supermarket, but it's much more rewarding to plant a tiny seed, take care of it, and watch it grow into something deliciously edible. You don't need to miss out if you haven't got any outdoor space—you can grow herbs, lettuce, tomatoes, and other vegetables in pots.

The Vegan SHOPPING LIST

Here are my storecupboard recommendations—keep all this at hand and you'll never run out of great plant-based meals to make.

FRUIT & VEGGIES

A wide variety of colorful vegetables and fruits.

DRIED STUFF

Red split lentils—For making a delicious dal in 15 minutes

Puy lentils—The earthy flavor and texture is amazing. A very "meaty" lentil, great for bolognese or burgers.

Quinoa—A complete plant-based protein—perfect for salads.

Rice—White, arborio, and brown.

FLOURS

Quality plain and self-rising flour and wholemeal—For fluffy flatbread or pizza bases.

Buckwheat & gram flour (made from chickpeas)—These are my favourite gluten free options.

Rye and spelt—Ancient grains with a nutty texture.

NUTS AND SEEDS

Seeds—Dry toast them to enhance their flavour.
Nuts—Essential for adding texture, protein and good fats.
Nut butters—Perfect healthy toast or porridge topper.
Tahini—For making hummus and dressings.
Ground almonds—To make the most delicious cakes.

CANS/JARS

Beans, chickpeas, and lentils—Keep a stock so you can make curries, chillis, dips, and salads in super quick time.
Tomatoes—The base for meals in minutes.
Coconut milk & coconut cream—For creamy curries and decadent desserts.

FRIDGE

Milks—There are some delicious plant based milks in shops now—try oat, almond, coconut, cashew, and soy.
Cheese—Shop-bought or homemade nut cheeses.
Tofu—Firm tofu for savory dishes, and silken tofu to make amazing desserts.
Coconut/plant based yogurt—Add a few tablespoons to curries, soups, and stews for a rich creamy texture and flavor.
Vegan butter & mayo
Cream—There are some amazing plant-based cream options available now.

FREEZER

Frozen peas—A brilliant ingredient. You can make an amazing dip or mash in minutes, and they add fantastic plant-based protein to curries.
Corn/edamame/other frozen veggies
Frozen fruit
Plant-based meat alternatives

OILS, SEASONING, SPICES, AND HERBS

Olive oil—Use for cooking and roasting.

Extra virgin olive oil—Adds delicious flavor for dressing, drizzles, dips and pestos.

Toasted sesame oil—For adding that toasted flavor to Asian dishes.

Coconut oil—Works well with Asian food.

Vegetable oil—for everyday cooking and cakes.

FLAVOR ENHANCERS

Seasonings

Salt/Sea salt flakes

Black Pepper

Lemon juice—Immediately enhances flavor. A squeeze of lemon can go a long way.

Stock—I absolutely love vegan bouillon - it works brilliantly in soup and stews.

"Nutritional yeast is the magic ingredient to make everything nutty, cheesy, and creamy"

SPICES

Indian spices: Cumin seeds, black mustard seeds, turmeric, cilantro, garam masala
Smoky flavors: Smoked paprika and ancho chilli
Middle Eastern: Fennel, caraway
Heat: Chili flakes, hot paprika, cayenne
Sweet: Cinnamon, ginger, allspice, mixed spice
General: Garlic powder

CONDIMENTS

Soy/Tamari—Adds savory saltiness.
Sriracha—Powerful chili sauce, lets you boost meals in seconds.
Rose harissa/harissa—Adds incredible depth of flavor and color.
Nutritional yeast—The magic ingredient to make everything nutty, cheesy, and creamy. It makes the perfect cheese sauce (with cashews), or just add it to pestos and sauces. It's a great source of B vitamins too.

FRESH HERBS

Mint—For dips, salads and desserts.
Cilantro—Great for Asian dishes.
Basil—Essential for creating batches of pesto.
Spinach—A versatile leaf that works in salads, curries, stews and pestos.
Thyme—Scrumptious in tomato dishes.
Dill—Lovely in slaws and salads.

Vegan in EVERYDAY LIFE

Being vegan means not eating meat, fish, or dairy. However, it's much more than that. It means avoiding causing harm or suffering to animals in any way. So how can you do that? It might be about what you wear, and the purchases you make. In what areas of your life can you make cruelty-free choices?

CLOTHES

Strict vegans don't wear the skins of animals, whether they were killed for them or not. So that includes leather, fur, and even wool—as it's possible that the shearing caused pain and suffering.

Things to avoid: Other types of fabric and fillings are also problematic—for example, silk is made by silkworms, which are a type of caterpillar. Silk is produced in their cocoons which are boiled with the pupae still inside, so the strands can be extracted. And feathers and down plucked from birds are commonly used for fillings for cushions, pillows, duvets, and in warm winter coats.

Good choices: Fair trade cotton, linen, bamboo, and "pleather" for shoes and bags.

SKINCARE

Although there are now many more vegan and cruelty-free brands of make up, body, and hair products with better labeling, there are still lots of products containing ingredients which have come from animals, or which have been tested on animals.

Things to avoid: Lanolin (from sheep's wool), shellac (from lac insects) or glycerine (from animal fats), collagen (from cows or marine), elastin or keratin.

Good choices: Cosmetics and skin care are usually clearly labeled as vegan or cruelty-free.

AT HOME

It's harder to make vegan choices at home, as so many things are manufactured with animal products or by-products.

Things to avoid: Furniture and houseware with hidden animal products within them, such as glue or dye.

Good choices: Check the labels of products you're buying, and also consider sustainable options at home, such as buying seasonal local produce and growing your own vegetables.

EATING OUT

Although the choices in cafés and restaurants have increased due to demand, it can still be hard to find a vegan option sometimes.

Things to avoid: Options that are flagged as vegetarian rather than vegan, vague "V" labels that are unclear, wait staff who can't explain whether something has animal products in it or not.

Good choices: Don't be afraid to ask for vegan or dairy free options, as most places should accommodate your needs. It's always a good idea to take your own healthy snack like nuts, fruit, or dips and bread.

Eat with the
SEASONS

These days, produce is available all year round, and we sometimes forget that fruit and vegetables used to only be available seasonally when they were ready to harvest.

Supermarkets now contain most foods through the year, and it's shipped in from warmer countries if it can't be grown locally.

This means that staples are available year round, and it's definitely more convenient. However, there's something joyful about anticipating produce coming into season—like strawberries, asparagus, tomatoes in the summer, and then root vegetables in the winter months.

WHY IT'S GREAT TO EAT SEASONALLY;

- **It tastes better and it's fresher.** Seasonal produce is grown closer to home, and has less time in transit which can cause a loss of flavor and nutrients.
- **You're doing something for the planet**—buying local and seasonal produce means less food miles. Food production and transport releases greenhouse gases like carbon dioxide and can use fossil fuels, which contribute to air pollution and global warming. So eating seasonally and locally can help cut down on environmental impact.
- **You can support local small businesses and farmers**—try to buy from markets or local shops.
- **Eating in season saves you money!** Prices usually go down on seasonal produce as there are less shipping and storing costs.
- **It's an opportunity to be creative.** If you cook with what's in season, it forces you to create dishes centred around the available produce.

Seasonal
FOOD CHART

Spring

PLANT	HARVEST
Brussels Sprouts	Asparagus
Carrots	Broccoli
Cabbage	Herbs
Herbs	Leeks
Lettuce	Mango
Onions	Pea shoots
Peas	Peas
Potatoes	Pineapple
Strawberries	Radishes
Tomatoes	Rhubarb

Summer

PLANT	HARVEST
Arugula	Beans
Broccoli	Blackberries
Carrots	Cherries
Cress	Eggplant
Kale	Garlic
Leeks	Nectarines
Pea shoots	Peas & mangetout
Potatoes	Peppers
Pumpkins	Plums
Strawberries	Tomatoes

Fall

PLANT	HARVEST
Beetroot	Apples
Broccoli	Carrots
Carrots	Herbs
Herbs	Leeks
Kale	Pears
Lettuce	Potatoes
Onions	Pumpkins
Radishes	Radishes
Spinach	Raspberries
Strawberries	Zucchini

Winter

PLANT	HARVEST
Blueberries	Brussel Sprouts
Beetroot	Cabbage
Broad beans	Cauliflower
Cabbage	Celery
Carrots	Cranberries
Cress	Kale
Garlic	Parsnips
Pea shoots	Pears
Radishes	Pomegranate
Lettuce	Chard

INGREDIENTS
Makes approx 5–6

. . . .

For the pancakes
1 ¼ cup self-rising flour

7 oz almond milk or
plant-based milk
of choice

4 tbsp maple syrup

1 tsp vanilla extract

Oil for frying if needed

Fillings
3 tbsp raspberries

3 tbsp blueberries

3 tbsp strawberries

Topping ideas
Plant based yogurt

Maple syrup/chocolate
sauce

Chopped nuts

Fruity pancake pockets

These light and fluffy pancakes are filled with juicy bursting fruit, like little pockets of goodness. All you need to do is spoon your pancake mix into the pan, pop some fruit on top, and then add some more pancake mix on top. Flip to cook the other side and envelope the fruit. There are loads of filling options—I also really like chocolate chips or peanut butter.

TO MAKE THE PANCAKES

1. Add the flour, almond milk, vanilla, and maple syrup to a large bowl and mix thoroughly to combine and form a thick batter.

2. Chop up the fruit into small pieces.

3. Add a little oil to a large non-stick pan.

4. Now spoon 2 tbsp of the mixture and spread it out to form a round pancake shape. You can probably fit 3 into the pan.

5. Immediately add 1 tbsp of the fruit to the top of pancakes.

6. Now spoon 1 tbsp more of the pancake mix on to the top of the fruit to cover.

7. Fry for 1–2 minutes until the underside is firm. You should see little bubbles forming on top.

8. Carefully flip the pancakes and then cook for another minute or so until the pancakes are cooked through and slightly golden.

9. Repeat with all the mixture and fruit and set aside on a plate.

New Year
REVOLUTIONS

The new year is an opportunity for fresh starts and to give yourself a focus on health. This could be in the form of exercising more, eating more fruit and vegetables, or perhaps signing up to Veganuary, the new yearly challenge to only eat plant-based food for the whole of January. (Try it—it's fun!)

For many people, winter festivities means there's been just a little bit too much indulgence in sweet treats and large celebratory dinners. So spring is the perfect time to step back and adjust the way you eat.

Remember—health doesn't come from simply eating healthily or doing the occasional bit of exercise alone—it's much more than that. Can you be really healthy if you are unhappy with friends, or feeling misunderstood? Things can get out of balance in your body if there's aspects of your life which you are unhappy with.

However, there are many ways of improving this and the new year is the perfect time to re-focus on your health and wellbeing. I'm not a health professional, but here are some things I've tried which have worked for me...

> **"Spring is the perfect time to step back and adjust the way you eat."**

EAT HEALTHIER

- **Eat more fresh vegetables and fruit**—Start by replacing a few meals a week with fresh home-cooked meals, and work from there.
- **Eat the rainbow**—Eating a broad spectrum of colorful fruit and vegetables means you get a variety of vitamins and nutrients to maintain a healthy diet. Try to include some colorful foods in every meal: add some berries to breakfast, snack on veg-based dips and pack the vegetables at lunch and dinner time.
- **Portion size**—You might be surprised how filling smaller portions can be.
- **Plan your menus and meals for the week**—This means you'll be sure to have healthy options on hand, rather than panic eating something unhealthy when you are hungry.
- **Sign up to Veganuary**—Get your friends and family involved and excited about plant-based foods.

FEEL FIT AND HEALTHY

- **Exercise should be fun!** Everything counts, including dancing, cycling, or yoga. Don't forget to speak to your GP if you have any concerns before starting a new exercise routine.
- **Try something new** or something you have forgotten about. How about trampolining or even tree-climbing?
- There are so many fantastic **online exercise classes and clubs**. Or just meeting friends for walks or a run outside can get you re-energized.
- **Sign up to an event** to keep you motivated.

LOOK AFTER YOUR MENTAL HEALTH

Our mental health is super important, especially during the recent challenging times. It's easy to think we are alone or no one will understand, but this is rarely the case. Here are some things that can help.

- **Talk about it**—The hardest step can sometimes be verbalizing your feelings and this can make us feel vulnerable. However, this is very often the first step to getting help or understanding your feelings.
- **Create a vision board** to display what you want to achieve and bring it to life. This will help focus your attention. Place it in a space where you see it often.
- **Get into nature**, stretch your legs, and feel the sun on your face. If you haven't been outside much, you might be surprised at how different it makes you feel.

Cucumber, lime, and mint cooler

INGREDIENTS
Serves 6–8

....

1 cucumber
Juice 2 limes
Handful of chopped mint leaves
1 liter chilled sparkling or still water
2 tbsp maple syrup

It's easy to make your own refreshingly sparkly cucumber, lime, and mint cooler—the perfect drink for warmer days in the garden, as it's a great thirst quencher. The fresh combination of cucumber and mint with zingy lime is just delicious. Still or sparkling water works well—make sure it's chilled beforehand.

1. Remove the skin of the cucumber using a peeler.
2. Now cut long and thin slices of the cucumber using the peeler, add to a large jug.
3. Squeeze in the juice of 2 limes.
4. Chop up the mint and add it to the jug, top up with the sparkling water and stir in the maple syrup.
5. You can serve immediately or store in the fridge until serving.

Niki's tip
Add in any of your favorite seasonal fruits—
I love raspberries or strawberries!

Bolognese flatbread pizza with tahini dressing

INGREDIENTS

For two medium flatbreads

For the bolognese sauce

1 red large onion
2 tbsp olive oil
4 cloves garlic
2 tsp smoked paprika
7 oz tomatoes
10 oz mushrooms
10 oz pack cooked puy lentils
2 tbsp sundried tomato purée or tomato purée
2 tbsp balsamic vinegar
1 tsp soy sauce
Twist black pepper
1 tsp sea salt

For the flatbread

13 oz self-rising flour
1 tsp baking powder
Pinch of salt
3 ozl water
3 tablespoon plant-based yogurt

For the tahini dressing

1 tbsp tahini
Pinch of salt
1 tbsp olive oil
Juice ½ lemon
2 tbsp water
Black pepper

Toppings

Fresh mint shredded
Chili flakes
Olive oil

These super fluffy flatbread pizzas are topped with a chunky lentil Bolognese topping, creamy tahini dressing and shredded fresh mint.

TO MAKE THE TOPPING

1. Finely chop the onion and slice the garlic.
2. Add the oil to a large pan and heat to a low to medium heat. Add the onion and fry for about 8–10 minutes until soft and browning. Add in the garlic and paprika and stir for another few minutes, then chop and add in tomatoes and mushrooms.
3. Cook down for 3–4 minutes then add the lentils, tomato puree, balsamic and soy. Stir and simmer for 5 minutes. Season well.

TO MAKE THE DOUGH

1. In a large bowl, stir the flour, baking powder and salt.
2. Now add the wet ingredients, mix thoroughly to combine and then transfer to a floured board.
3. Knead for a few minutes for a springy dough.

TO COOK

1. Heat a large griddle pan or frying pan to medium.
2. Divide the dough into two, then roll out the first flatbread.
3. Pop it on the griddle pan and allow to cook and char a little, then flip to cook on the other side.
4. Repeat with the second section of dough.
5. Keep the flatbreads warm on a plate covered with a clean cloth.

TO MAKE THE DRESSING

Add all the ingredients to a jar and mix to combine.

TO SERVE

Top the pizzas with the Bolognese, tahini dressing, and fresh mint.

Niki's tip
You can use the flatbread bases and add whatever you like—tomato and pesto are delicious, or hummus and roast vegetables.

EQUIPMENT

Cocktail sticks
Heart-shaped cookie cutters
Rolling pin

INGREDIENTS

4 oz ground almonds
2 tbsp oats of choice
3 tbsp cacao powder
Pinch of sea salt flakes
3 tbsp peanut butter
2 tbsp melted coconut oil
1 tsp vanilla extract
4 medjool dates pitted
3.5 oz vegan chocolate
1 tsp coconut oil

Toppings

Chopped pistachios

Freya's love hearts

Show someone you love them with these cute heart-shaped chocolate cookies.

These hearts are intensely chocolatey and there's no need for baking—just blend them up in a food processor, cut into little heart shapes, freeze so they don't crumble when you pop the stick in, then envelop them in melted chocolate. Delicious!

TO MAKE THE LOVE HEARTS

1. In your food processor, blend together the ground almonds, oats, cacao powder, a pinch of salt, peanut butter, vanilla, dates, and melted coconut oil to form a sticky mix.

2. Form the mix into a ball in your hands then pop on a chopping board. Roll the mix out 1cm thick and use heart shaped cookie cutters to create the hearts. Re-roll until you've used up all the mix.

3. Arrange them on a lined baking tray and freeze for 30 minutes to firm up.

4. Break up the chocolate and add to a small pan with the coconut oil. Very gently heat on a low heat until the chocolate is melted. Don't overstir.

5. Remove the hearts from the freezer and place a cocktail stick into the center of each heart, then dip in the melted chocolate.

6. Add them back to the tray and then sprinkle pistachios over the top.

7. Transfer back in the fridge to firm up. Store in the fridge.

Niki's tip
You can top with any crushed nuts. Seeds or dried flowers are also lovely!

Hoisin mushroom lettuce cups

INGREDIENTS

4 spring onions

2 tbsp toasted sesame oil

3 cloves garlic

1 tsp grated ginger

16 oz mushrooms

1 red pepper

8 oz mixed seeds— sunflower, pumpkin

2 tbsp soy sauce

4 tbsp hoisin sauce

2 tbsp tomato purée

Pinch of chili

Pinch of salt & black pepper

Little gem leaves

7 oz cooked rice

2 tbsp sesame seeds

Impress your friends with these tasty bites! My hoisin mushroom lettuce cups are super easy to make and the filling is delicious—juicy mushrooms in a tasty hoisin soy sauce, loaded onto rice and encased in cute little gem leaves. It's fun sharing food and perfect for parties.

TO MAKE THE MUSHROOM FILLING

1. Finely chop the mushrooms and red pepper and add to a bowl.
2. Slice the spring onion and garlic, and grate the ginger.
3. Add the sesame oil to a medium pan. Add the spring onions and fry for 6–8 minutes until soft and browning.
4. Add in the garlic and ginger and cook for a further minute. Transfer the chopped mushrooms and peppers to the pan, and fry until soft, around 4–5 minutes.
5. Now add the seeds, soy sauce, tomato purée, and hoisin sauce, and stir to combine.
6. Cook for a further 2–3 minutes and finally add the chili flakes. Set aside.

TO SERVE

Top the lettuce with a spoonful of rice then a spoonful of mix. Top with sesame seeds.

Niki's tip
Why not use your own home-grown lettuce leaves?

INGREDIENTS

For the chat masala

2 lb new potatoes
2 tbsp olive oil
1 tsp cumin seeds
1 tsp fennel seeds
½ tsp chili flakes
1 tsp garam masala
1 tsp turmeric
½ tsp ground cilantro
½ tsp garlic granules
½ tsp salt

For the green sauce

4 tbsp coconut yogurt
1 bunch of cilantro
1 bunch of mint
½ tsp garlic granules
½ lime juice
Pinch of salt
Pinch of chili flakes

To serve

2–3 tbsp Indian snacks such as Bombay Mix
2–3 tbsp pomegranate seeds
¼ red onion, finely diced
2 tbsp mango chutney
1 handful of fresh cilantro and mint

Crispy new potato chat masala

I'm a bit obsessed with crushed potatoes—soft and fluffy on the inside and super crispy on the outside. My lightly spiced Indian street food version is next-level. If that's not enough, I've added layers of tasty extras: a creamy herb sauce, crunchy Indian snacks, mango chutney, and pomegranate—yum!

TO MAKE THE CHAT MASALA

1. Pre-heat the oven to 180°C.
2. Boil the potatoes in salted water for 10–15 minutes. You want them to be cooked through but still hold their shape when lightly crushed.
3. Drain the potatoes, allow to cool a little, then place on a large chopping board and lightly crush using a fork.
4. Mix the masala mix in a jar, then transfer the potatoes to a large baking tray.
5. Drizzle over the masala mix and toss to cover the potatoes.
6. Bake for about 40 minutes—halfway through, squish the potatoes a bit with fork.

TO MAKE THE GREEN SAUCE

Chop up the cilantro and mint then add all the ingredients to a jar to combine.

TO SERVE

Top the potatoes with the green sauce, indian snacks, pomegranate, red onion, mango chutney, and fresh herbs.

Em's strawberry & vanilla cream coconut cake

INGREDIENTS

For the cake

1 ¼ cup coconut milk drink

1 tbsp cider vinegar

1 tsp vanilla

4.5 oz light olive oil

1 ⅔ cup plain flour

¾ cup desiccated coconut

4 oz ground almonds

6 oz superfine vegan sugar

Zest of 1 lemon

1 tsp baking powder

½ tsp baking soda

For the filling

¾ cup plant-based double cream

2 tbsp superfine vegan sugar

4 tbsp strawberry jam

Fresh strawberries

Mint

Make your mom or a loved one this stunner of a cake! It's a light and sweet coconut sponge filled with strawberry jam and cream, topped with thick and creamy plant-based whipped double cream and fresh strawberries—what a dream. I've made this cake for family and friends many times now, and it's always a winner.

TO MAKE THE CAKE

1. Preheat the oven to 350°F.
2. In a bowl, stir the coconut milk, cider vinegar, vanilla, and oil.
3. In a separate large bowl, add the flour, sugar, baking powder, coconut, and lemon zest. Stir to combine.
4. Now add in the liquid to the dry mix. Stir thoroughly to combine.
5. Pour the mixture into a lined cake tin, and place into the oven to bake for roughly 35–45 minutes or until the middle is cooked. Check by inserting a cocktail stick into the middle—if it comes out clean it's cooked.
6. Once baked, remove from the oven and allow to cool completely.
7. Very carefully cut in half by slicing through the middle.

TO MAKE THE FILLING

1. Add the cream and sugar to a large bowl.
2. Whisk using an electric whisk or immersion blender until the cream is stiff.
3. Spread the jam on top of the first layer of the cake then spread cream on top. Carefully replace the top half of the cake.

TO SERVE

1. Spread the remaining cream on top, then add the strawberries and mint.
2. Keep the cake in the fridge until it's ready to serve.

Nutrition
NEEDS

If you are new to a vegan lifestyle, you might be concerned whether your diet will cover all your nutritional needs. The good news is that a healthy and balanced vegan diet should provide you with almost everything you need for good health. However, you do need to be mindful of getting what you need in terms of key nutrients.

There are some key vitamins and minerals you need to be aware of when embarking on your vegan journey.

VITAMIN B12

Vitamin B12 keeps your heart healthy, helps to make red blood cells and helps prevent nerve damage, and is found in meat, fish, eggs, and dairy. Many vegans don't get enough B12.

The good news is there are good sources in fortified foods such as breakfast cereals, plant milks and yogurts, vegan spreads, and some meat substitutes.

However if you are concerned about your intake, you'll need to speak to your GP. They may take a blood test to check your levels and refer you to a dietitian to discuss how you can get enough from your diet.

CALCIUM

A healthy, balanced, and varied vegan diet rich in whole grains, pulses, nuts, seeds, and green leafy veg should provide enough calcium, and choosing calcium-fortified milks and yoghurts will help to ensure that you're getting what you need.

IRON

Make sure you're getting enough iron—many young people struggle to get enough iron in their diets, especially if they're not eating meat. Dark green leafy vegetables like watercress, nuts, wholegrains, beans and dried fruits are all good sources of iron. Breakfast cereals and wheat are often fortified with iron too.

OMEGA 3 FATTY ACIDS

Diets rich in omega 3 fatty acids may be helpful for protecting our heart health and memory.

The main source of EPA and DHA omega 3 fatty acids is oily fish, but our bodies can convert some plant-based sources of ALA into EPA and DHA after we've eaten them.

You can get some ALA from nuts and seeds, vegetable oils, some soya products like tofu and soya milk, and some green leafy vegetables. Some foods are also enriched with omega 3s—check the label.

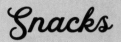

Homemade veggie chips with sweet chili hummus

INGREDIENTS
Serves 4–6

....

For the veggie crisps
1 sweet potato

1 large parsnip

1 potato

1 carrot

1 tsp garlic granules

Pinch of sea salt

2 tbsp olive oil

For the sweet chili hummus dip
11 oz cooked chickpeas drained

1–2 tbsp sweet chili sauce/jam

1 tsp garlic granules

2 tbsp olive oil

Juice ½ lemon

2 tbsp plant-based yogurt

½ tsp salt

Pinch of black pepper

Chili flakes—optional

Did you know that root vegetables make delicious homemade chips? They are much healthier than shop-bought chips, and super tasty. Make sure you slice the vegetables as thinly as possible as this will help them cook and crisp up nicely. You can then add any spices you fancy!

TO MAKE THE CHIPS
1. Pre-heat your oven to 350°F.
2. Very carefully, slice the vegetables as thinly as you can.
3. Add the veggies to two large baking trays, then toss in the garlic granules, salt, pepper, and olive oil.
4. Bake for 40–45 minutes, turning occasionally.
5. Keep an eye on them and remove any crispy ones if they cook faster than others.

TO MAKE THE HUMMUS
Add all the ingredients to a food processor and blend until smooth and creamy.

TO SERVE
Dip the veggie crisps in the dip.

Niki's tip
You can use shop bought dips, but why not whip up a batch of homemade hummus flavoured with sweet chili—delicious!

INGREDIENTS

¾ cup oats of choice

⅔ cup medjool dates pitted

2 tbsp maple syrup

Pinch of sea salt

1 cup rice krispies

3 tbsp vegan butter

2 tbsp maple syrup

1 tbsp cacao powder

3.5 oz vegan chocolate

1 tbsp coconut oil

Tilly's Easter caramel rice krispie bites

These rice krispie cakes are my niece Tilly's favorite, and she's a tough judge! They remind me of baking with my mom when I was little, getting my hands all sticky and making the buttery crispy bites. It's incredible just how delicious these little squares are, considering the simple ingredients. They make the perfect homemade Easter treat.

TO MAKE THE RICE CRISPY BITES

1. Add the oats to a food processor and blend to a fine crumb. Now add the dates, maple syrup, and sea salt, and blend again until you get a chunky dough.
2. Line a small tray with baking paper, then transfer the oat mix. Squish down with your hands to cover the base and push into the corners.
3. Melt the butter on a low heat with the maple syrup and cacao in a small saucepan until everything is combined.
4. Add the rice krispies to a bowl and then pour over the chocolate sauce. Stir to combine so all the rice krispies are coated.
5. Spoon them over the oat base. Press into the corners with a spoon.
6. In the same saucepan, break up the chocolate and add along with the coconut oil and heat very gently on a low heat until melted. Don't overstir.
7. Now pour over the rice krispies to cover. Pop in the fridge to firm up—at least 2 hours.
8. Store in the fridge.

Niki's tip
You can fill the filo tarts with anything you like—I love dates, caramel, jam, chocolate squares or fruit.

INGREDIENTS

For the coronation tofu bagels

12 oz firm tofu, drained

½ tsp curry powder or garam masala

2 tbsp mango chutney

3 tbsp yogurt (or vegan mayo or sour cream)

½ tsp turmeric

½ tsp garlic powder

1 tbsp lemon juice

2 tbsp nutritional yeast

2–3 tbsp raisins

Pinch of salt

Twist of black pepper

4 bagels

Cress for serving

INGREDIENTS

For the banana jam peanut butter filo tarts

½ packet filo pastry

3 tbsp sunflower oil (spray)

½ jar peanut butter

½ jar cherry jam

2 large ripe bananas

Coronation tofu bagels & banana jam peanut butter filo tarts

Create an afternoon tea to be proud of with these tasty coronation tofu bagels and easy-to-make jammy banana peanut butter filo tarts. Both can be packed up, so are perfect for picnics.

TO MAKE THE CORONATION TOFU BAGELS

1. Finely dice the tofu and add it to a bowl.
2. Now mix the dressing ingredients in a bowl then add to the tofu and mix to combine.
3. Add the raisins and salt and pepper. Mix again.
4. Toast the bagels and top with the coronation tofu mix. Add the cress.

TO MAKE THE BANANA JAM PEANUT BUTTER FILO TARTS

1. Preheat the oven to 350°F.
2. Remove the filo pastry from the fridge then roll out and cut the pastry in half. Now cut out into six squares. Then put in a pile.
3. Lightly spray a 12 hole muffin tin with oil spray.
4. Place a square of filo over one of the muffin cups, spray lightly with oil, add another at a slight angle, spray again and do the same with the last square.
5. Slice up the bananas.
6. Add a tbsp of peanut butter to each case, then 1 tsp of jam, then top with 4 slices of banana.
7. Now place a square of pastry over the bananas as a lid, press in gently, spray with oil, then fold in the edges of the pastry over the lid and press down.
8. Give each pastry a final spray of oil, then add a sprinkle of brown sugar and bake them for 25 minutes or until golden and crisp.

SUMMER

INGREDIENTS
Makes approx 4–5

....

1 onion
1 tbsp oil
1 cup frozen peas
1 cup frozen edamame
1 tsp garlic powder
2 tbsp nutritional yeast
Juice of ½ a lemon
Handful dill
Handful fresh mint
1 tsp baking powder
½ tsp salt
Black pepper
⅔ cup self-rising flour
Toasted seeds

For the corn salsa

6 oz canned corn, drained
2 tomatoes, chopped
2 spring onions
2 tbsp fresh mint
Pinch of salt
Pinch of chilli flakes
1 tbsp olive oil
Juice of ½ a lemon

Edamame & pea fritters with corn salsa

These vibrant green fritters made from peas and edamame are delicious just as they are, but I like them loaded with a fresh corn salsa for some lovely summery vibes.

TO MAKE THE FRITTERS

1. Chop up the onion into small pieces.
2. Now add them along with the oil to a frying pan. Fry on medium for 7–8 minutes until soft. Turn off the heat.
3. Defrost the peas and edamame by adding them to a sieve and running them under warm water until they are defrosted.
4. Now add them along with the cooked onions, garlic salt, nutritional yeast, lemon juice, fresh herbs, baking powder, salt, and pepper. Blend until a rough paste is formed, then add the flour and blend again briefly.
5. In a frying pan, add a little oil, then scoop up 1 heaped tbsp of the mix and carefully dollop into the pan, flattening with the spoon to shape into a circle.
6. Fry for 4–5 minutes, or until golden and crispy, then flip over to cook for another 2–3 minutes on the other side. Don't try to flip them too soon! They're much easier to turn once they've turned golden and crispy underneath.

TO MAKE THE SALSA

1. Chop the onions and tomatoes into small pieces.
2. Transfer to a bowl along with the other ingredients, and stir to combine.

TO SERVE
Top the fritters with the salsa and seeds.

Niki's tip

You can also make a batch, allow to cool, wrap up, and store in the fridge to take for packed lunches or picnics.

Grow your own TOMATOES

The taste and smell of homegrown tomatoes is hard to beat, and being able to pick juicy sweet ripe tomatoes straight off your own plant is just wonderful. The great news is that they are easy to grow from either seed or young plants, and there are some incredible varieties available now.

1. SOW YOUR SEEDS

- Sow your seeds in spring to plant in early summer for the best results.
- To grow from seed you will need:
  - A recycled fruit punnet or biodegradable pots
  - Compost
- Fill each punnet with compost, then add some water.
- Sow 6 seeds per punnet, then top with a little more compost.

2. GROW THE SEEDLINGS
- The tomato seedlings should have appeared after two weeks.
- When they reach 8 cm tall, carefully transfer them into individual larger biodegradable pots with drainage holes.
- Place in a warm, sunny spot to grow.

3. TRANSPLANT THE PLANTS
- Transplant your seedlings to a large flowerpot filled with compost. Water them regularly.
- When it's warm enough, place them in a sunny spot outside to grow. The plants might need to be secured with a pole if they grow high!

4. GET PICKING
- You will see lots of flowers appearing, each of which will then become a little tomato.
- Pick when red and ripe.
- They're ready to wash and eat right away, or to create something delicious with!

TURN OVER for the ideal tomato salsa recipe...

INGREDIENTS
Serves 2–4

6 ripe tomatoes
1 red onion
3 cloves garlic, unpeeled
2 tbsp olive oil
Pinch of sea salt
Twist of black pepper
Pinch of chili flakes
Handful of cilantro
or mint
Juice of ½ a lime
or lemon
½ tsp cumin seeds
½ tsp black pepper
½ tsp sea salt

To top
Extra virgin olive oil
Fresh herbs

Roast tomato salsa

I love this version of salsa—it's a little different to the usual raw variety, as you roast the tomatoes, onion, and garlic first which adds loads of flavor. It also works really well with slightly squishy tomatoes!

TO MAKE THE SALSA

1. Preheat oven to 390°F.
2. Slice the tomatoes into quarters and add them along with the onion and garlic to a baking tray. Drizzle with olive oil and season with salt and pepper.
3. Roast for about 25–30 minutes, or until soft. Set aside and allow to cool a little.
4. Add everything (including the juices) to the food processor—squeeze the garlic out of its skin.
5. Now add all other ingredients and blend to a chunky salsa.
6. Top with extra virgin olive oil and fresh herbs.

Niki's tip
It's perfect as a dip, spread on toast, tossed into pasta, or even used to top rice.

INGREDIENTS

1 long loaf or large ciabatta

12 oz jar roast peppers, drained

For the basil & arugula pesto

2 tbsp pine nuts

4 tbsp seeds—a mix of sunflower and pumpkin

1 clove garlic, peeled

Juice ½ lemon

3 tbsp nutritional yeast

¼ cup fresh arugula

¼ cup fresh basil

2 tbsp olive oil

½ tsp salt

¼ cup water

For the carrot slaw

1 large carrot

2 spring onions

2 tbsp dill or mint

2 tbsp garlic mayo or mayo

Squeeze of lemon

Pinch of salt

Handful of arugula

2 tbsp vegan mayo

Picnic layered sandwich with roast pepper, arugula pesto & slaw

When the sun is shining, why not pack up a picnic and get into the park or even the back yard? My layered picnic sandwich is a meal in one—fresh basil and arugula pesto topped with roast peppers, carrot and dill slaw, fresh arugula, and a big smear of creamy mayonnaise. Sandwich it all together, wrap, then pop in the fridge until you're ready to go.

TO MAKE THE PESTO
Add all the ingredients to a food processor and blend to combine.

TO MAKE THE SLAW
1. Grate the carrot and slice the spring onions.
2. Add them to a bowl and now add the dill, mayonnaise, lemon juice, and salt.
3. Stir to combine.

TO SERVE
1. Carefully slice the loaf in half lengthways.
2. For the bottom layer, spread a good layer of pesto over the base of the bread.
3. Now add the roast peppers and then top with the carrot slaw and arugula leaves.
4. Finally, spread mayonnaise over the top of the loaf.
5. Press firmly down and then wrap in clingfilm.
6. Place in the fridge until you are ready to take on your picnic.

Niki's tip

Other delicious flavor combinations include hummus and roast veggies, or sundried tomatoes and vegan cheese.

INGREDIENTS
Serves 6–8

....

For the filling

1 onion
3 cloves garlic
1 tbsp smoked paprika
1 zucchini
3.5 oz mushrooms
5 large ripe tomatoes
3 ⅓ cups cooked lentils
½ jar sun dried tomatoes
1 tbsp soy sauce
1 cup vegetable stock
1 tsp sea salt
Black pepper

For the cheesy béchamel sauce

2 tbsp vegan butter
4 tbsp plain flour
2 cups almond milk
3–4 tbsp nutritional yeast
Big pinch of sea salt
Twist of black pepper

For the pesto

3.5 oz pine nuts or sunflower seeds
3 cups raw spinach
1 ½ cup basil
12 oz frozen peas, defrosted
Juice ½ lemon
1 tsp sea salt
1 clove garlic
3 tbsp nutritional yeast

6 Lasagne sheets

Summer green lasagne

My summer green lasagne is a bit of a crowd-pleaser. It has layers of tasty lentils, "cheesy" sauce, pasta sheets, and then a gorgeous green pesto.

TO MAKE THE TOMATO & LENTIL FILLING

1. Finely chop up the onions, slice the garlic, and then roughly chop the mushrooms, zucchini, and tomatoes.
2. Add your oil and onion to a wide bottom pan and fry gently on a low heat for around 10 minutes until soft and browning.
3. Add the garlic and spices and fry for 30 seconds more then add the mushrooms and zucchini and fry for a further couple of minutes.
4. Add the tomatoes, lentils, sun dried tomatoes, soy, and stock to the pan and cook on a low heat for 10 minutes.
5. Add the salt and black pepper to the pan and simmer for a further 2 minutes.

TO MAKE THE CHEESY BÉCHAMEL SAUCE

1. Add the butter to a frying pan and melt on a low heat then add the flour. Stir to combine well.
2. Next, add the almond milk and nutritional yeast. Simmer for 5 minutes, stirring constantly to ensure no lumps form.
3. Season well and remove from the heat.

TO MAKE THE PESTO

Add all the ingredients to your food processor or high-speed blender and blend until everything is combined to the texture you prefer. You may need to scrape the sides down a few times.

Niki's tip

Swap the zucchini for squash or sweet potato in the winter, and why not try some wild garlic instead of spinach in the pesto?

TO MAKE THE LASAGNE

1. In a medium roasting dish (I used a 10-inch one), layer the tomato veggie filling, then 3 lasagne sheets, then half the cheese sauce, top with pesto, then another layer of tomato veggie mix, 3 lasagne sheets, then the remaining cheese sauce (make sure to cover the edges of the lasagne sheets), and finally top with pesto.

2. Cover with foil and bake for 30 minutes, then uncover and cook for 10 more minutes on 350°F.

Summer fruit smoothie ice cream

INGREDIENTS
Serves 4–6

....

18 oz mixed summer fruits, frozen or fresh

2 large ripe bananas frozen bananas

3 oz coconut cream

7 oz coconut milk

4 tbsp maple syrup

For the frozen version
Add 2 tbsp plant-based yogurt

Toppings
Toasted coconut
Sesame seeds
Chopped nuts

This is next-level banana "nice cream"—the coconut adds extra creaminess, making it super delicious. And then the mixed summer fruits (either frozen or fresh) make the whole experience super-fresh and bursting with flavor.

TO EAT RIGHT AWAY

1. Blend all the ingredients in a food processor until smooth and creamy then scoop out to serve as soft serve.
2. Add any toppings.

TO EAT LATER

1. Blend all the ingredients together until smooth.
2. Pour into one or two freezer bags. Press the air out and seal.
3. Freeze overnight or until completely frozen.
4. When you want to serve, remove from the freezer and break into pieces. Pop into a food processor along with the plant-based yogurt, and blend until smooth and creamy.
5. Scoop out to serve, and add toppings.

Niki's tip
You can add absolutely any fruit you like and definitely go crazy with the toppings!

INGREDIENTS
Makes 4 skewers

....

For the jerk marinade
3 tsp jerk spice

1 tsp vegan sugar

1 tsp sea salt flakes

1 tsp sweet paprika

3 tbsp olive oil

11 oz block firm tofu, sliced into large cubes

1 red pepper

1 zucchini

12 mushrooms

For the beans and rice
8-oz can black beans, drained

1 cup cooked rice of choice

1 ripe mango

2 spring onions

Big handful fresh mint and cilantro, shredded

Dressing
Juice of 1 lime

2 tbsp extra virgin olive oil

1 tsp maple syrup

Pinch of sea salt flakes

Pinch of black pepper

Jerk BBQ skewers with mango & black bean rice

These tasty and fun BBQ veggie and tofu skewers have a punchy jerk flavor and make the perfect family meal. You can cook on the BBQ or bake—both ways are delicious!

TO MAKE THE MARINADE
Mix the spices in the jar with the oil and sugar.

TO MAKE THE SKEWERS
1. Cut up the zucchini, peppers, and tofu into cubes.
2. Put the veggies in one tub and the tofu in another. Cover both in the marinade and mix carefully, making sure it's all covered.
3. Allow to marinate for at least 30 minutes.
4. When ready to cook, add the veggies and tofu to the skewers. You can either bake in the oven or add to a BBQ.

TO BAKE
1. Pre-heat your oven to 350°F.
2. Line a large baking tray with tin foil. Place the skewers on top and bake for about 25 minutes until cooked through.

ON THE BBQ
Carefully place the skewers onto the BBQ and cook for 20–25 minutes—turning occasionally.

TO MAKE THE RICE
1. Peel and cut the mango into cubes. Slice the spring onion.
2. Now add all the ingredients to a bowl and mix to combine.
3. To make the dressing, add all the ingredients to a jar and mix to combine. Now mix into the rice.

TO SERVE
Serve the skewers with the rice and a squeeze of lime.

Niki's tip

If you're using wooden skewers, you will need to soak them in water for at least 15–30 minutes before threading the vegetables.

Veganism and
HEALTH

Some people still think it's impossible to be healthy when you are a vegan. There are still pre-conceived ideas that you will lack protein or other nutrients.

This isn't the case—you just need a little planning to ensure you eat a balanced diet to achieve optimum health. Here are some easy to ways to incorporate more plant based protein and other essential nutrients into your diet!

FROZEN PEAS

These are my go-to staple and I always have a few bags in the freezer. It means you can grab handfuls to add to curries, soups or salads, or make a quick pea and mint dip in seconds.

CHICKPEAS

Not only are chickpeas rich in iron, fiber and other nutrients, they can form the base of multiple meals including curries, hummus and blondies. You can also get chickpea flour (also known as gram flour) which is made from dried baby chickpeas, and can be made into crêpes or flatbreads.

NUTS AND SEEDS

Sprinkle toasted nuts and seeds on top of everything! It adds crunch, plus lots of healthy fats and protein.

GET YOUR B VITAMINS

Since Vitamin B12 isn't found in most vegan food, you'll need to ensure you're eating foods fortified with it, such as fortified dairy-free milks. If you're concerned, speak with a GP or dietitian about supplementing your diet. Read more about B12 on page 34.

RAINBOWS OF VEG

Eating a broad spectrum of colourful fruit and vegetables means you get a variety of vitamins and nutrients to maintain a healthy diet.

Phytonutrients are found in plant foods like vegetables, fruits, nuts, seeds, legumes and whole grains. Teas, herbs and spices contribute to the colour of plant foods.

By eating foods from every colour group, you get a wide variety of these beneficial properties.

INGREDIENTS

For the roast tomatoes
1 cup cherry tomatoes
Splash of olive oil
Pinch of sea salt

For the cheesy peas
3 ½ cups frozen peas, defrosted
1 tbsp olive oil
½ lemon juice
1 tsp sea salt
1 clove garlic
50g pine nuts, toasted
3 tbsp nutritional yeast

Pasta of choice

Toppings
Pine nuts
Chilli flakes
Extra virgin olive oil
Herbs

Optional
Big handful of basil or mint

Cheesy pea pesto pasta with roast tomatoes

This all-round crowd-pleaser of a dish can be whipped up in minutes—it's a perfect healthy storecupboard staple, as you can use frozen peas and dried pasta. Juicy roast cherry tomatoes are a gorgeous summery ingredient, but you can add some sun-dried tomatoes or eat just as it comes. This easy-peasy pasta sauce doubles as a delicious dip—it's perfect spread on toast.

Eat more peas! Green peas are a legume and are a great source of vegetable protein and fibre. They are fairly low in calories and contain several vitamins, minerals and antioxidants.

TO ROAST THE TOMATOES
1. Add the cherry tomatoes to a baking tray and toss them in 1 tbsp of olive oil.
2. Bake on a medium heat for 30 minutes or until soft and browning a little. Set aside.

TO MAKE THE CHEESY PEAS
Add all the ingredients to a food processor and blitz until you get a chunky sauce.

TO MAKE THE PASTA
Cook the pasta as per the instructions on the pack. Toss the pasta in the pea sauce, then top with the roast tomatoes and any additional toppings.

INGREDIENTS
Serves 4

....

For the peppers
4 red peppers
2 tbsp olive oil
Big pinch of sea salt

For the rice
1 tbsp olive oil
6 spring onions
3 cloves garlic
8 sundried tomatoes, chopped up
2 tsp smoked paprika
2 tbsp sundried tomato paste
1 cup cooked rice of choice
3 oz green olives, chopped
½ tsp sea salt
6 tbsp mixed seeds
Juice ½ Lemon

For the roast tomatoes
1 ¼ cup cherry tomatoes
Splash of olive oil
Sea salt

Toppings
Fresh herbs: basil, thyme, or dill

Options
Vegan pesto
Toasted bread

Tomato rice stuffed peppers with roast tomatoes

This is such a summery meal, packed with juicy roast summer veggies! The sweet roast peppers make the perfect bed for the tasty tomato rice and bursting roast tomatoes. They make a brilliant accompaniment for a barbecue feast, or to pack up and take on a picnic.

TO ROAST THE PEPPERS AND TOMATOES
1. Pre-heat your oven to 350°F.
2. Cut the peppers in half and remove the seeds.
3. Add the peppers to a large baking tray and drizzle with oil and season.
4. In another pan, add the cherry tomatoes and drizzle with oil and season.
5. Bake both for 30 minutes, then remove from the oven. Set aside in the tray.

TO COOK THE RICE
1. In the meantime, chop the spring onions and slice the garlic, then add to a large pan.
2. Fry the spring onion in olive oil until soft then add the garlic. Fry for a further minute or so.
3. Now add all the remaining ingredients and stir to combine. Cook for 5 minutes. Set aside.

TO SERVE
1. Spoon the rice filling into the baked peppers and bake for another 10 minutes.
2. Remove from the oven.
3. Top with roast tomatoes and herbs.

Niki's tip
For extra deliciousness I love to top with some pesto!

Make your own PLANTERS

You don't need to buy expensive pots to start growing your own plants and herbs. Many things around the home which usually get thrown away can be recycled into pots to grow seedlings and plants in.

FOR SEEDLINGS

You can use toilet roll tubes to grow seeds in. Fill with compost, and nestle the seeds inside.

Used fruit and veggie punnets also make fantastic seed trays!

FOR PLANTS

You can make planters for larger plants from a variety of everyday things; try upcycled large tin cans, old buckets, or hessian bags.

GROW YOUR OWN CHILIES!

Chilies are fun to grow at home and quite straightforward even from seed—here's what you need to do!

1. Sow your seeds in the middle of spring to make sure you get a crop for summer.

2. Fill a small pot with compost and sow a few seeds on top and water.

3. Pop on a warm windowsill.

4. When the seedlings are 1 inch tall, transfer each seedling to its own pot filled with multi-purpose compost. Place in a sunny spot and water regularly.

5. Move the plants into larger pots when they are 5 inches tall. Support with a bamboo cane if they start to lean.

6. Plant them in May in your homemade planter or a grow bag.

7. Place in a sunny spot outside and water regularly.

8. You'll get fully-grown chilies within two to four months of sowing.

Niki's tip

The red pesto is amazing—use for pasta, rice, veggies, or in sandwiches.

4 slices of bread of choice

For the red pesto
8 sundried tomatoes in oil, drained

12-oz jar roasted red peppers, drained

1 ½ cup fresh basil

6 oz pine nuts, toasted

1 clove garlic

4 tbsp nutritional yeast

3 tbsp extra virgin olive oil

Big pinch of sea salt

Pinch of black pepper

Pinch of chili

Squeeze of lemon juice

For the toasted seeds
3 tbsp sunflower seeds

3 tbsp sesame seeds

½ tsp sea salt flakes

Topping
1 avocado

Fresh cress

Dill

Open sandwich with red pesto, avocado, & cress

This simple open sandwich is perfect for brunch or lunch—the red pesto is the star of the show. It's similar to a classic basil pesto, but with added roast peppers and sundried tomatoes. The toasted salty seeds are also a must—they add incredible crunch and savory umami flavours—be warned, they are completely addictive!

TO MAKE THE PESTO
1. Add all the ingredients to a mini chopper or food processor and blend to a chunky paste.
2. Transfer to a jar.

TO MAKE THE SEEDS
1. Add to a dry pan and gently toast on a medium heat until lightly brown. Be careful not to burn them.
2. Stir in the salt, then transfer to a jar with a lid.

TO SERVE
Toast bread then spread generous amounts of pesto on top. Add sliced avocado, toasted seeds and fresh herbs.

Cherry peanut butter blondies

INGREDIENTS

For the blondies

1 cup cooked chickpeas, rinsed and drained

4 tbsp ground almonds

⅓ cup self-rising flour

5 tbsp brown vegan sugar

1 tsp baking powder

Pinch of sea salt

4 tbsp peanut butter

1 tsp vanilla extract

4 tbsp maple syrup

3 tbsp light veg oil

1 tsp apple cider vinegar

3 tbsp plant based milk

3.5 oz fresh cherries

3.5 oz vegan chocolate, broken into small chunks

For the toppings

Cherries, pitted

Chopped nuts

These blondies are based on a recipe I created a few years ago, and they have a secret ingredient—chickpeas! I know it sounds weird, but they create a lovely squidgy texture. With the chickpeas, almonds, and peanut butter, these little treats are high in protein.

1. Pre-heat the oven to 350°F and line a small baking tray with parchment paper.
2. Pit and roughly chop up the cherries.
3. Add all the ingredients apart from the chocolate and cherries to a food processor, and mix until smooth and creamy.
4. Transfer the batter to a large bowl and stir in the cherries and chocolate chunks. Then spoon into the baking tray, smooth out evenly, then sprinkle with toasted nuts and a few more cherries.
4. Bake for 25-30 minutes. Allow to cool **completely** before removing from the tray and slicing. Enjoy!

INGREDIENTS
Serves 1–2

....

¼ cup water with 2½ tsp instant coffee

1 large frozen banana

10 ice cubes

¾ cup oat milk

2 tsp cacao powder

½ tsp vanilla extract

2 tbsp maple syrup

1 scoop vegan vanilla ice cream

Toppings
1–2 scoops vegan vanilla ice cream

Iced mocha float shake

If you love iced coffee like me, then you'll love this. It's pretty special—creamy bananas, chocolatey coffee, vanilla ice cream—heaven. Perfect for sharing ... or drinking all by yourself!

1. Make the coffee and allow to cool.
2. Add all the ingredients to a food processor and blend until smooth & creamy.
3. Transfer to a large glass (or two), and top with vanilla ice cream.

FALL

Caramelized pear French toast

INGREDIENTS

For the caramelized pears

3 pears, sliced

1 tsp cinnamon

3 tbsp maple syrup

6 slices bread of choice—I like chunky white or sourdough

1½ cups plant-based milk

4 tbsp maple syrup

1⅔ cup self-rising flour

1 tsp baking powder

1 tbsp cinnamon

½ tsp allspice

Pinch of sea salt

1 large ripe banana

3 medjool dates pitted and chopped

Oil, for frying

Other optional toppings

Plant-based yogurt

Nut butter

Maple syrup

Toasted walnuts

French toast, I hear you say? Oh yes! Layers of fluffy and sweet banana toast topped with caramelized pears, with a drizzle of maple and some creamy yogurt. The pears add a delicious seasonal element. This recipe has been taste tested by the very discerning Miss Ayla.

TO MAKE THE CARAMELIZED PEARS

1. Pre-heat your oven to 350°F.
2. Add the pears to a baking tray then drizzle with maple and cinnamon. Toss to combine. Bake for approx. 25–30 minutes until soft and caramelized.
3. In a bowl, whisk together the milk, maple syrup, flour, baking powder, cinnamon, allspice, and salt.
4. Mash up the banana, and add it along with the dates to the mix. Stir well.

TO MAKE THE FRENCH TOAST

1. Pour some of the batter into a shallow dish (with sides), now add a slice of bread, then lift or flip the bread over to make sure both sides are coated.
2. Heat a little oil in a large frying pan (medium heat) then add a bread slice and cook for a few minutes per side, until golden brown. Repeat with the other slices.

TO SERVE

1. For a stack of French toast—place the first slice on a plate, spread over peanut butter and then place the next slice on top. Repeat.
2. Top the third slice with the pears and yogurt and a sprinkle of nuts and maple. Or you can just serve one slice topped with everything!

Niki's tip

The key to getting a fluffy French toast is making sure the batter is really thick and sticks to the sides of the bread and coats it really well. Encase the bread in the pancake-like batter and watch it fluff up.

Making
PRESERVES

Have you ever thought about making your own jams, chutneys, or pickles? Preserving is an ancient technique for keeping excess produce and leftovers, but in the modern world with fridges, freezers, and everything being available all year round, we have mostly lost this yearly tradition.

The process of preserving the glut of summer fruits and vegetables by pickling, fermenting, and making preserves was historically essential to ensure food supplies over the winter months. The need for this is long gone in most Western countries—however, there are many environmental reasons for giving it a go. For example, it creates less food waste, reduces your food miles, and saves money.

If you grow your own fruit and veggies, you'll know that crops tend to be ready all at once and you can be left with way too much for personal use at home, so preserving comes in very handy. Plus there's something magical about the process of preserving, especially when you have grown the produce yourself.

JAMS

The sweet treat we spread on toast is made from fruit and sugar, and also often contains pectin which gives it a thick texture.

Niki's tip:
Jams and chutneys make lovely edible gifts.

CHUTNEY

Chutneys can be made with sweet ingredients like fruits, but with added spices and vinegar turning the condiment into something spicy and fragrant.

Niki's tip:
Chutneys are perfect for adding to salads or toast.

Niki's tip:
I love to make pickles and add them to sandwiches, or top curries or dals with them.

PICKLING

Pickling uses an acid solution such as vinegar to preserve produce by killing or inhibiting the growth of the bacteria that cause food to go off.

FERMENTING

With fermenting, the process involves a metabolic change that converts sugars to acids, gases or alcohol.

Fermented foods tend to have a sour taste due to the lactic acid produced by the fermentation process. Popular fermented foods include yogurts, kimchi, sauerkraut, wines and beers.

Niki's tip:
Fermented non-alcoholic foods may be beneficial to gut health!

Make your own
JAM & CHUTNEY

Why not try to make your own jam or chutney with your homegrown fruit and veggies? It will mean you could be enjoying your produce throughout the year, plus they make wonderful presents for friends and family.

But don't worry if you haven't grown your own—you'll also find that supermarkets tend to have cheaper produce in the summer months, so you can still try making your own preserves.

The easiest and quickest way to make jam is with chia seeds. Use the gelling power of these tiny little seeds to transform fruit into a low-sugar, spreadable jam in about 20 minutes!

Jam

Blackberry & blueberry chia jam

INGREDIENTS

1 cup blackberries
1 cup blueberries
2 tbsp chia seeds
3 tbsp maple syrup
Juice of ½ a lemon

1. Add the berries, maple syrup and chia to a small saucepan.
2. Cook on a low heat for 10 minutes, stirring occasionally to ensure all the chia seeds are mixed in and everything is combined.
3. Allow to cool and store in a glass jar in the fridge. It will last 4–5 days.

Chutney

Tomato chutney

INGREDIENTS

9 cups red onions
2 lb tomatoes
2 cooking apples
5 garlic cloves
1 red chili
1.5-inch piece of ginger
½ cup brown vegan sugar
5 oz red wine vinegar
1 tsp smoked paprika
1 tsp salt

This is a fantastic recipe for using up excess summer tomatoes, and it tastes delicious on toast with some cashew cheese.

1. Slice the onions, chop the tomatoes up, peel, core, and chop up the apples, and slice the garlic and red chili.
2. Peel and grate the ginger.
3. Add all the ingredients into a large pan and bring to a gentle simmer, stirring often. Simmer for 1 hour, then bring to a gentle boil so that the mixture turns dark, jammy, and has thickened.
4. Transfer to sterilized jars while the chutney is still warm. Allow to cool before sealing.

Foraging in
NATURE

Foraging in nature has always been a way of collecting food and medicinal herbs for humans. These days we mostly rely on supermarkets and pharmacies, but foraging is making a resurgence, and has been gaining popularity for a few years now. It's a fun and rewarding experience to find pieces of "nature's candy" in hedgerows, beaches, and woodlands.

FORAGING DOS AND DON'TS

- **DO** make sure you minimize damage to the environment.
- **DON'T** take more than you plan to consume.
- **DON'T** take anything from plants you're unsure of—they may be endangered or poisonous.
- **DO** stick to paths and avoid private property, and take care not to damage areas you are collecting from.
- **DON'T** uproot the whole plant—only pick leaves and berries.
- **DON'T** pick fungi without an expert, as it's easy to mistake poisonous species for safe ones.
- **DON'T** eat raw leaves unless you're 100% sure they're safe.
- **DO** remember to seek permission if needed.

WHAT TO FORAGE

Month	Where to find them	How to use them
JANUARY		
Chestnuts	Woodland	
Crabapple	Countryside	Crabapple jelly
Hawthorn berries	Hedgerows, woodland	
FEBRUARY		
Nettles	Hedgerows, woodland	Teas, pesto, soups
Wild garlic	Woodland	Pesto, soups, stews
MARCH		
Gorse flowers	Heaths and grassland	Eat the flowers only
Hawthorn leaves	Hedgerows, woodland	Salads, teas
APRIL		
Mallow leaves	Hedgerows	Salads
MAY		
Sorrel leaves	Woodland	Salads
JUNE		
Elderflowers	Hedgerows	Cordial, desserts
Honeysuckle flowers	Hedgerows	Eat fresh
Dog Rose petals		Syrups
JULY		
Whinberries	Heathland and moorland	Pies and crumbles, sauces
Wild strawberries	Hedgerows	
AUGUST		
Blackberries	Hedgerows	Jams/compôtes, eat fresh
Elderberry—ripe fruit	Hedgerows	Jelly, crumbles, jams
Hazelnut	Hedgerows, woodland	Eat raw, pesto, salads
SEPTEMBER		
Rosehip	Hedgerows	Syrups
Sloes	Hedgerows	Syrups, gin
Wild raspberry	Hedgerows	Eat fresh
OCTOBER		
Sweet chestnut	Woodland	Roasted
Walnut	Woodland	Sprinkles and dukkah
NOV/DEC		
Pine	Woodland	Eat the seeds

INGREDIENTS

For the flatbread

1 ½ cups self-rising flour

1 tbsp vegan sugar

1 tsp baking powder

2 tbsp cacao powder

3 oz water

3 tbsp plant-based yogurt

For the chocolate

2 tbsp smooth peanut butter

4 tbsp coconut oil

2 tbsp cacao powder

4 tbsp maple syrup

For the berries

2 cups berries of choice

Splash water

1 tbsp maple

Toppings

Coconut yogurt

Fresh mint

Chocolate pizza with gooey berries

Are you up for some chocolate pizza? This pizza has a chocolate base topped with sticky peanut chocolate sauce, gooey berries, and creamy coconut yogurt.

TO MAKE THE FLATBREAD

1. In a large bowl, add the flour, sugar, baking powder, cacao, and salt. Stir to combine.
2. Now add the water and yogurt, mix thoroughly to combine, and then transfer to a floured board. If you need to add a bit more water or flour then do so.
3. Knead for a few minutes, until you get a springy dough.

TO COOK

1. Heat a large griddle pan or frying pan to medium.
2. Divide the dough into four then roll out the first flatbread.
3. Pop it on the griddle pan and allow to cook and char a little on that side, then flip to cook on the other side. Repeat for the other flatbreads.
4. Keep the flatbreads warm on a plate covered with a clean cloth.

FOR THE BERRIES

Add the berries, maple syrup, and water to a small pan and heat gently on a stove until the fruit starts to break down and go all gooey.

FOR THE CHOCOLATE

1. Add the coconut oil to a small pan, and very gently heat until melted.
2. Now add the remaining ingredients and stir to combine.

TO SERVE

Top the pizza bases with lots of chocolate sauce, warm berries, and yogurt.

Black bean jackfruit baked chimichanga wraps

INGREDIENTS

8 oz black beans, drained
8 oz jackfruit, drained
15-oz jar roast peppers, drained
1 tsp garlic powder
1 tsp ground cumin
1 tbsp smoked paprika
Pinch chili flakes
2 tbsp sundried tomato purée/tomato purée
2 tsp vegan worcester sauce
3 tbsp BBQ sauce
Juice of ½ a lime
½ tsp salt
Twist of black pepper
5 oz vegan cheese, grated
6 wraps of choice
Oil spray

For the Pico de Gallo sauce

10 cherry tomatoes
½ red onion
Handful cilantro
1 tbsp olive oil
Handful mint
Pinch of chili
Juice of ½ a lime
Pinch of salt

For serving

4 tbsp plant-based yogurt

The tasty filling inside these wraps is super easy to make. Just mix everything together, add them to the wraps, and bake until they become crispy on the outside and oozing and warm on the inside. Top with the fresh Pico de Gallo sauce for extra zing!

TO MAKE THE FILLING

1. Open and drain the beans, jackfruit, and roast peppers.
2. On a chopping board, roughly chop up the jackfruit and roast peppers, then add them along with all the other ingredients to a large bowl and stir to combine well.
3. Lay out your wraps then place equal amounts of the filling along the middle. Top with vegan cheese, if using.
4. Fold the sides in toward the filling, then fold the larger sides around the filling to form your wrap.

TO COOK THE WRAPS

1. Pre-heat your oven to 350°F.
2. Place each wrap into a baking tray, bake nestled next to each other, and then spray the top with oil.
3. Bake for 15–20 minutes until the wraps are crispy.

TO MAKE THE PICO DE GALLO

1. Finely chop the onion, tomatoes, cilantro, and mint.
2. Add all the ingredients to a bowl and stir to combine.

TO SERVE

Top the chimichangas with Pico de Gallo sauce and plant-based yogurt.

Niki's tip

You can use any beans you want and can swap the jackfruit for roast veggies if you like—squash or sweet potato work really well.

INGREDIENTS
Approx. 18 servings

2 Weetabix

3 oz plant-based milk

½ cup oats of choice

1 apple

1 small carrot

2 ripe bananas

4 tbsp maple syrup or sweetener of choice

4 tbsp mixed dried fruit

4 tbsp chopped hazelnuts

1 tsp baking powder

1 tsp ground ginger

1 tsp cinnamon

1 tsp vanilla essence

Apple & carrot cake cookies

These cookies make a brilliant quick and tasty breakfast or a healthy portable snack. They include some super healthy ingredients ... but they taste like apple and carrot cake. And they have a secret breakfast ingredient—the breakfast cereal Weetabix! This adds lots of fiber along with the fruit, carrots, and dried fruits.

TO MAKE THE COOKIES
1. Pre-heat your oven to 350°F.
2. Add the Weetabix to a large bowl with plant-based milk. Allow to sit for a minute or so to soften.
3. Grate the apple and carrot.
4. Add all the ingredients to a large bowl, and stir thoroughly to combine.
5. Line a baking tray with baking paper, then scoop out heaped tablespoons of the mix and place on the tray. Squish them down to flatten a little, then bake for 20 minutes. Allow to cool a little before gobbling them down!

Niki's tip
Apples are at their best in fall through to spring.

Chickpea kati roll

This special Indian spiced kati roll is so delicious—tasty spiced warm chickpeas all wrapped up with squishy crêpes. Top with some cooling yogurt and herbs, wrap and devour!

INGREDIENTS

For the crêpes

1 ¾ cup plain flour

½ tsp sea salt

½ tsp baking powder

1 tsp apple cider vinegar

1 ½ cup plant-based milk

For the curry

1 tbsp coconut oil or light olive oil

1 large onion, diced finely

3 cloves of garlic, sliced

1 tsp cumin seeds

1 tsp garam masala

1 tsp turmeric

1 cup cherry tomatoes

1 tbsp tomato purée

3 ⅓ cups spinach

1 can chickpeas, drained

2 tbsp coconut or plant-based yogurt

Sea salt and ground black pepper, to taste

Toppings

Chili flakes

Cilantro and mint, for serving

Plant-based yogurt

TO MAKE THE CRÊPE BATTER

1. Mix the dry ingredients in a large bowl.
2. Add in the olive oil, vinegar, and plant-based milk, and whisk thoroughly until you get a thick batter. Stir in the herbs. Set aside for 15 minutes.

TO MAKE THE CURRY

1. Add the oil to a large frying pan and heat to a medium heat. Add in the diced onion and fry for about 8–10 minutes until soft and browning, then add the garlic and spices—stir for another few minutes, then add in the chopped tomatoes and tomato purée.
2. Cook for a further 4–5 minutes then chop the spinach and add it to the pan.
3. Allow the spinach to wilt down for 2–3 minutes then add the chickpeas and yogurt. Season.

TO MAKE THE CRÊPES

1. Add a little oil to the base of a medium non-stick frying pan. Add ⅓ cup of the batter to the pan and swirl around so you get an even crêpe.
2. Cook on a medium heat for approximately 1–2 minutes until there are bubbles in the flatbread and you can lift over to flip easily.
3. Flip and cook on the other side for 30 seconds to a minute.
4. Remove from the pan and place on a plate. Cover with a clean cloth to keep warm. Repeat the process with the rest of the batter.
5. Load the crêpes with the spiced chickpeas, yogurt, and fresh herbs.

Niki's tip

I love to use chickpeas but you could use lentils, roast sweet potato, or vegan meat alternatives.

Pumpkin harissa hummus

INGREDIENTS
Serves approx. 4

....

2 cups pumpkin
or squash
1 tbsp olive oil
Pinch of salt and pepper

1 cup cooked chickpeas
1 clove garlic
2 tbsp tahini
2 tbsp olive oil
1 tsp harissa
2 tbsp plant-based
yogurt
Pinch of chili flakes
½ tsp sea salt
Black pepper
Juice of ½ a lemon

Toppings
Extra virgin olive oil
Chili flakes
Smoked paprika

What can you do with leftover Halloween pumpkin? Make some hummus, of course! This is the perfect way to use things up—just roast and blend to a creamy, dreamy dip with some chickpeas, tahini, and a little spicy harissa for warmth.

1. Pre-heat your oven to 350°F.
2. Peel and cut up the pumpkin or squash, place on a baking tray and drizzle with a little oil, salt, and pepper.
3. Roast for 40–50 minutes until tender. Allow to cool.
4. Now add all the ingredients to your food processor and blend until smooth and creamy.
5. Add toppings to serve.

Niki's tip
You don't need to wait for Halloween—this recipe works just as well with roast squash or sweet potatoes.

Cheesy squash carbonara with fried mushrooms

I can only claim this is loosely related to a carbonara—but it's the best way I could think of to describe the creamy delicious sauce encasing the pasta! It's made from roast squash, onion, and garlic all whizzed together with some smoky paprika and nutritional yeast—it's super tasty, and doubles as a dip if you have any leftovers.

INGREDIENTS
Serves 4

1 medium squash, peeled
1 onion, chopped
1 garlic bulb
1 tbsp olive oil
½ tsp salt
¼ tsp ground pepper
20 oz spaghetti or other pasta of choice

For the sauce
2 tbsp tomato purée
¾ cup almond milk
2 tbsp olive oil
3 tbsp nutritional yeast
1 tsp smoked paprika
1 tsp sea salt
Pinch of black pepper

Toppings
12 oz mushrooms, sliced
1 tbsp olive oil
Pinch of salt and black pepper
3.5 oz plant-based bacon (optional)

TO PREPARE THE SAUCE
1. Pre-heat the oven to 350°F.
2. Peel the butternut squash, carefully chop into small cubes, then add to a baking tray.
3. Add the onion. Toss with olive oil, salt, and pepper and spread out on the tray. Now add the garlic bulb.
4. Roast for about 40 minutes or until it's cooked and golden brown. Remove the garlic after 20 minutes.
5. Reserve a quarter of the roast squash.

TO MAKE THE SAUCE
1. Add the roast squash, tomato purée, paprika, salt, almond milk, olive oil, nutritional yeast, and the peeled roast garlic to a food processor. Blend until you get a creamy sauce.
2. Add a little water for a looser consistency, then transfer to a saucepan.
3. Sauté the mushrooms with the oil in a pan. Fry until soft, then season with salt and pepper.
4. Cook the pasta following pack instructions, and drain.
5. If you're adding vegan bacon, cook according to the pack instructions.
6. Add the pasta to the sauce in the pan and stir and heat gently.
7. Top with the roast squash, mushrooms, and bacon.

Niki's tip
You don't need to add plant-based bacon, but it will make this recipe even more delicious.

Get
SWAPPING!

Are you missing some non-plant foods you used to love? Here are some vegan swaps to inspire you.

NUTTY FOR CHEESE

Cheese is very often one of the main stumbling blocks for people considering going vegan. There are now lots of new vegan "cheese" products out there, but it's still very hard to replicate dairy cheese exactly.

Try making nut cheese instead, which is a natural and less processed alternative. It's very easy to make, and you can make a quick version by blending soaked cashews with nutritional yeast flakes (de-activated yeast which has a "cheesy" flavor and contains vitamin B12, which many vegans lack). This can be eaten right away or aged to make a crust and give it a more intense flavor.

MEATY SUBSTITUTES

If you're looking for something to replicate the texture and taste of meat, you can find everything from burgers to "chicken" pieces made from ever more sophisticated soy or pea proteins. They have their place, and are convenient options! But here are some great "meaty" vegetables to load up on during a transition to a plant-based diet which might help curb any craving for meat.

- **Mushrooms**—Many varieties have a lovely "meaty" texture. Especially the incredible king mushroom which can be marinated and griddled to charred perfection. Try serving them with grilled tomatoes and scrambled tofu for a delicious brunch!
- **Jackfruit**—Super popular as it's a brilliant flavor carrier, and the texture is somewhat similar to pulled pork or shredded chicken.
- **Cauliflower, celeriac, and broccoli "steaks"**—I love roasting these amazing vegetables and serving them as a healthy centerpiece dish.

CHOCOLATE

You shouldn't feel like you are missing out at all with chocolate. Quality dark chocolate with high cacao content is usually dairy-free—as chocolate is made from cocoa beans which are then dried and fermented, its naturally vegan. It's only the process of adding milk along with sugar which makes chocolate non-vegan. Many chocolate producers now add coconut or plant-based milk instead of cow's milk, and there are lots of amazing dairy-free chocolate bars and truffles out there. For baking, swap cocoa for raw cacao in chocolate desserts and cakes, and swap chocolate chips for cacao nibs.

CREAM AND YOGURT

Plant-based alternatives for cream have improved dramatically, with whippable options now widely available. Finding thick and creamy greek yogurt and sour creams made from oats, nuts, soy, or coconut is also easy. For me, coconut is the dream ingredient for adding creaminess and richness instead of cream or yogurt. It adds a huge amount of texture, flavor, and creaminess to vegan food, and a little goes a long way.

Spiced corn 'ribs'

This autumnal treat is a brilliant, healthy, but fun snack—crispy, sweet, lightly spiced, and bursting with flavor. Dip it into my roast tomato salsa or some sweet chili—delicious! The trickiest bit is slicing the corn into four. You will need a sharp knife and a steady hand—and maybe someone to help if needed.

TO MAKE THE CORN RIBS
1. Pre-heat your oven to 350°F.
2. Cutting the corn is quite tricky—you need to stand it up vertically with the wider part against the chopping board, and chop in half, then chop those halves into quarters. It's very tough, so you might need a hand.
3. Transfer to a baking tray.
4. Add all the rub ingredients to a jar and mix to combine.
5. Brush the rub over the chopped corn to coat.
6. Bake for about 35–40 minutes or until charred and curling.

Harissa bean burgers with sweet potato fries

The perfect family meal—lightly spiced harissa bean burgers with sweet potato fries! I think the best bit about burgers is when you add all your favorite toppings—creamy yogurt mint dip, tomato salsa and pickles—yum!

INGREDIENTS
Makes 12 burgers

For the wedges
2 sweet potatoes
2 white potatoes
Big pinch of sea salt
1 tsp garlic granules
2 tbsp olive oil

For the burgers
1 tbsp olive oil
1 red onion
3 garlic cloves
1 red pepper
½ tsp chili flakes
1 tsp ground cumin
1 tbsp smoked paprika
1–2 tbsp harissa paste
3 tbsp tomato purée or tomato ketchup
13.5 oz black beans, drained
3 cups cooked Puy lentils (freshly cooked and drained, or a pouch)
5 tbsp plain flour
Sea salt and freshly ground black pepper

To serve
Buns of choice
Tomatoes
Tomato salsa (Page 49)
Pickles
Yogurt/mint dip (4 tbsp yogurt, shredded mint, pinch salt, squeeze lemon juice)
Little Gem lettuce leaves

TO MAKE THE WEDGES
1. Pre-heat your oven to 350°F.
2. Cut the sweet potatoes and potatoes into wedges then add to a large roasting pan with the olive oil, salt, and garlic powder. Roast for 20 minutes, then turn. Continue to roast for a further 20 minutes or until the veggies are golden brown.

TO MAKE THE BURGERS
1. Slice the onion, garlic, and peppers.
2. Add the oil and onion to a frying pan and cook for 6–8 minutes to soften. Now add the garlic and red pepper and cook for a further 2–3 minutes.
3. Add the spices and stir to combine, cook for a further minute, then set aside.
4. Add the black beans and veggies to a food processor along with the harissa and tomato paste. Blend to a smooth-ish paste.
6. Transfer to a large bowl along with the lentils, flour, and salt and pepper. Stir to combine.
7. In a large non-stick frying pan, heat a little oil and spoon a heaped tablespoon of the mixture into the pan and flatten and spread out to a round burger shape.
8. Repeat for each burger. Remember to leave enough room to flip the burgers!
9. Fry for 2–3 minutes each side until lightly brown.
10. Set aside on a plate and repeat with the remaining mixture. Fill the buns with the lettuce leaves, the burgers and your choice of toppings.

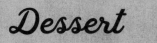

Black forest cupcakes

INGREDIENTS
Makes 12

. . . .

For the dry mix
¾ cup white self-rising flour
¾ cup ground almonds
1 tsp baking powder
½ cup cacao powder
1 cup light brown vegan sugar

For the wet mix
1 tsp vanilla extract
1 cup almond milk
3 oz vegetable oil
1 tsp apple cider vinegar

For the filling
Black cherry jam

For the topping
Plant-based double cream
Fresh or glacé cherries
Dark chocolate, grated

These cute and deliciously decadent little cupcakes are a fun nod to the classic 1970s dessert in cupcake form. The lovely rich chocolate cake is filled with cherry jam, and topped with whipped plant-based cream. With a cherry on top!

TO MAKE THE CHOCOLATE CUPCAKES
1. Pre-heat the oven to 350°F, and line a muffin tray with 12 cases.
2. Mix the dry ingredients in a large bowl.
3. Mix the almond milk, vanilla, vegetable oil, and cider vinegar in a jug, then pour into the dry mix.
4. Stir until smooth.
5. Divide the mixture equally between the 12 muffin cases and bake for 20 minutes.
6. Use a skewer to test that the middle of the cupcakes come out clean—if it does, they're done.
7. Leave to cool then cut small holes in the center of the cupcakes. You can use a small sharp knife to hollow out the centers.

TO FILL & DECORATE
1. Spoon some cherry jam into the holes. Set aside.
2. Now whip the plant-based double cream according to the pack instructions.
3. Top the cupcakes with the whipped cream and a cherry.
4. Grate some chocolate on top.
5. Store in the fridge.

INGREDIENTS

For the fruit

3 small apples, peeled, cored, and chopped into small cubes

3 medium pears, peeled, cored, and chopped into small cubes

4 tbsp mixed dried fruit

½ cup water—more if needed

1 tsp ground cinnamon

4 tbsp brown vegan sugar

For the peanut butter crisp

1 cup oats of choice

3 tbsp sunflower seeds

4 tbsp chopped nuts

3 tbsp plain flour

Pinch of sea salt

1 tsp baking powder

5 tbsp maple syrup

5 tbsp chunky peanut butter

Apple, pear, & peanut butter crisp

This is made from lovely warm and sweet fruit, topped with an absolutely delicious peanut butter and oat crispy topping. Eat it warm out of the oven with creamy ice cream or coconut yogurt, or scoop into a bowl and pour over cold plant-based milk for a delicious breakfast option.

TO MAKE THE FRUIT

1. Preheat the oven to 350°F.
2. In a saucepan, combine the apples, pears, water, cinnamon, dried fruit, and sugar. Cover and cook on a medium heat, stirring occasionally, for 15 minutes or until the fruit softens and breaks down.
3. Now transfer the fruit to the base of a flan dish.

TO MAKE THE TOPPING

1. Mix the oats, flour, baking powder, chopped nuts, seeds, and salt together in a bowl.
2. Now add in the peanut butter and maple syrup. Mix thoroughly until you get a crumb (get your hands involved). Then cover the fruit with the finished mixture.
3. Put in the oven and bake at 350°F for 25 minutes—it's ready when the topping is golden and crispy. Remove from the oven and allow to cool a little.
4. Top with vegan ice cream or yogurt.

Niki's tip

You can use any seasonal fruit—I love cherries, strawberries, or even peaches or nectarines in the summer.

Niki's tip

Top your hot chocolate with vegan whipped cream, chocolate sauce, or vegan marshmallows.

Ultimate hot chocolate three ways

Is there anything better than wrapping your hands around a warm and steaming mug of hot chocolate? Here are three delicious versions for you: a classic rich and creamy hot chocolate, a lovely chocolate orange version, and a mint choc chip version with choc chips melted into the hot chocolate.

INGREDIENTS
Serves 1

1

For the creamy rich hot chocolate

1 cup plant-based milk
2 tbsp coconut cream
2 tbsp cacao powder
2 tbsp maple syrup
Tiny pinch of salt
1 tsp vanilla extract

2

For the chocolate orange hot chocolate

1 ¼ cup plant-based milk
2 tbsp cacao powder
2 tbsp maple syrup
Pinch of ground cloves
1–2 tsp orange extract

3

For the mint choc chip hot chocolate

1 cup plant-based milk
1 tbsp cocoa powder
2 tbsp vegan choc chips
2 tbsp coconut cream
2 tbsp maple syrup
½ tsp peppermint extract

To make the hot chocolate

1. Choose your hot chocolate from the three options to the left.
2. Add all the ingredients to a saucepan and heat gently on a medium heat.
3. Whisk while heating to remove any lumps.
4. Pour into a mug and top with vegan cream if you like.

The best sticky ginger cake with lemon glaze

INGREDIENTS
Serves 16

Dry ingredients
2 ½ cups self-rising flour

1 ¼ cup ground almonds

2 tsp baking powder

½ tsp baking soda

5 tsp ground ginger

2 tsp allspice

1 tsp cinnamon

¾ cup brown vegan sugar

½ tsp salt

Wet ingredients
5 oz sunflower oil

5 oz golden syrup

½ cup treacle

1 cup boiling water

For the lemon glaze
½ cup vegan icing sugar, sifted

Juice of ½ a lemon

When I was a little girl, my favorite treat was Jamaican Ginger Cake—the deep stickiness at the base of the cake was so dreamy. I think I've done a pretty good job of replicating it here. It's sticky and sweet with just the right amount of ginger.

TO MAKE THE CAKE
1. Pre-heat the oven to 350°F.
2. Grease a medium high-sided cake tin and line with baking paper.
3. Add all the dry ingredients to a large bowl and mix to combine thoroughly.
4. Now add the golden syrup, treacle, sunflower oil, and boiling water to a jug, and whisk until combined.
5. Pour into the dry ingredients and mix well.
6. Pour the batter into the tin and bake for about 25 minutes, or until a skewer inserted into the center comes out clean.
7. Allow to cool completely, then remove from the tin.

TO MAKE THE LEMON GLAZE
1. Combine the icing sugar in a bowl with the lemon juice and mix until smooth.
2. Drizzle the glaze over the cake, then cut into squares and serve.

Niki's tip

As an alternative to the tangy lemon glaze, serve warm with creamy vanilla vegan ice cream.

WINTER

Posh beans with avocado & pan-griddled bread

INGREDIENTS

For the beans

1 tbsp olive oil
1 large red onion
2 cloves garlic
1 tbsp smoked paprika
1 tsp cumin seeds
1 tbsp sundried tomato paste
1 cup cherry tomatoes
1 cup black beans
Pinch of chili flakes
3 oz water
½ tsp sea salt
Pinch of black pepper

For the bread

2–4 slices sourdough
2 tbsp extra virgin olive oil
Sprinkle of sea salt flakes

Toppings

Plant-based yogurt
Avocado

Smoky beans are like a big hug in a bowl! My posh beans are ridiculously good, rich, and delicious black beans with a hint of chili—they're the ultimate comfort food, and perfect for brunch or a quick meal. You could scoop up with some fresh bread, but it's even better when you make this crispy pan-griddled bread with it!

FOR THE BEANS

1. Chop up the onion, mince the garlic, and chop up the cherry tomatoes.
2. Add the oil and onion to a wide-bottom pan and fry gently on a low heat for around 10 minutes until soft and browning. Add the garlic and spices and fry for 30 seconds more.
3. Add the tomatoes, sundried tomatoes, and tomato paste to the pan and cook for 5–10 minutes until the tomatoes have softened.
4. Now add the beans and water and cook on a low heat for 5 minutes.
5. Finally add the salt, black pepper, and chili flakes.

FOR THE PAN-GRIDDLED BREAD

1. Heat a griddle pan to medium.
2. Brush some extra virgin olive oil onto both sides of the bread. Sprinkle with sea salt. Add to the pan and toast on one side then flip until toasted on the other side.

TO SERVE

Top the beans with avocado and creamy yogurt. Serve with the griddled bread.

Niki's tip

You can swap the black beans for chickpeas or butter beans.

Staying healthy in WINTER

Staying healthy in winter is a little harder than summer, as the cold environment makes it easier for bugs to multiply and spread as you are spending more time indoors. We can make sure our bodies have a better chance of fighting off infections by eating healthily and smartly. Here are some easy ways to add healthy ingredients to your dishes.

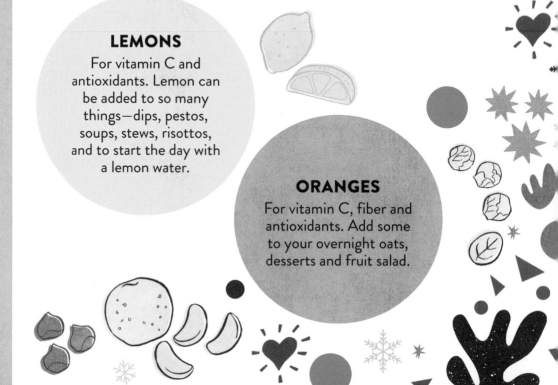

LEMONS

For vitamin C and antioxidants. Lemon can be added to so many things—dips, pestos, soups, stews, risottos, and to start the day with a lemon water.

ORANGES

For vitamin C, fiber and antioxidants. Add some to your overnight oats, desserts and fruit salad.

GINGER

Ginger is a diaphoretic, meaning it promotes perspiration, so it is used in some cultures to treat fevers and colds. Add fresh ginger to curries, smoothies, and cakes. Add ground ginger to cakes, cookies, and oats.

TURMERIC

An antioxidant which contains curcumin. It can support the immune system and may have anti-inflammatory properties. Add both fresh and ground to Asian dishes, porridge, and cookies.

CINNAMON

Cinnamon contains antioxidants. Add to your breakfast oats, desserts, curries, fruits, and smoothies.

TURN OVER for my health boosting porridge recipe...

INGREDIENTS

For the porridge

½ cup jumbo oats

1 tbsp peanut butter

½ cup plant-based milk of choice

½ cup orange juice

1 tsp ground ginger

¼ tsp ground turmeric —optional

½ tsp cinnamon

1 tsp vanilla essence or powder

1–2 tbsp maple syrup

Toppings

Peanut butter

Plant-based yogurt

Health-boosting porridge

Breakfast is the best meal of the day in my opinion! Firstly, it's an opportunity to eat delicious food and secondly, to get in some good nutrients at the start of the day. This is especially so in the winter months, when your immune system gets more challenged and you need to fight off colds and viruses.

TO MAKE THE PORRIDGE

1. Add the oats, milk, orange juice, and spices to a small saucepan. Simmer on a low heat, stirring continuously for a few minutes until the porridge has absorbed the milk but is not too dry.
2. Turn off the heat and stir in the maple syrup, peanut butter, and more plant-based milk if needed.
3. Top with toppings of your choice.

My immune-boosting porridge packs in some fantastic ingredients to help support your body's natural defenses:

Orange juice—Contains vitamin C, fiber and antioxidants.
Ginger—Diaphoretic, promoting perspiration.
Turmeric—Contains antioxidants, can support the immune system, and may have anti-inflammatory properties.
Cinnamon—Contains antioxidants.

INGREDIENTS

For the soup

1 large red onion

2 tbsp olive oil

1 tbsp curry powder

1 tsp smoked paprika

3 cloves garlic

2 parsnips, cubed

1 large sweet potato, peeled and cubed

1 cup red lentils, rinsed

6 cups vegetable stock

3 tomatoes, sliced

Big pinch of sea salt to taste

Pinch of black pepper

Pinch of red chili flakes

3 tbsp coconut cream or yogurt

For the croutons

½ a baguette or 2 slices of chunky bread

3 tbsp olive oil

2 tbsp nutritional yeast

½ teaspoon salt

1 teaspoon garlic powder

Pinch of black pepper

Toppings

Plant-based toppings

Chili flakes

Spiced parsnip, sweet potato, & lentil soup

This soup has everything I love: warming spices, a hint of chili and a little coconut cream for depth of flavor and creaminess. It's a lovely winter warmer packed full of seasonal veggies and lentils—healthy and delicious.

TO MAKE THE SOUP

1. Finely chop the onion and slice the garlic.
2. Now add the oil to a large frying pan and heat to a medium heat. Fry the onion for 8–10 minutes until soft and caramelizing.
3. Now add the curry powder and paprika and stir to combine. Add in the garlic and stir for another few minutes.
4. Meanwhile, peel and cube the sweet potato and parsnips.
5. Now add the parsnips, sweet potato, tomatoes, lentils, and stock. Cover and simmer for 15–20 minutes until the lentils are tender.
6. Add the coconut cream, salt, pepper, and chili to taste.
7. You can either serve it chunky, completely smooth, or slightly blended. Just whizz up with a hand blender—it's best if you leave some texture in the soup.

TO MAKE THE CROUTONS

1. Preheat the oven to 350°F.
2. Mix the oil, nutritional yeast, salt, and garlic powder in a large bowl.
3. Toss with the bread (I prefer to use my hands to really get all the bread coated).
4. Transfer to a baking tray and bake for 10–15 minutes, until golden brown and crispy.

TO·SERVE
croutons,
... based
ogurt ...
chili.

The perfect plant-based PARTY

Follow these tips and you'll create an amazing foodie gathering!

1 GET PLANNING

Part of the fun is planning the event, seeking out ingredients, and just being creative. You can have fun with a theme and make the whole party look beautiful with table settings and decorations. Getting organized is usually the hardest part—that's why you should ensure you get the timings right and make sure everything is done on time.

2 PLAN YOUR MENU

Create a food theme—this gives you something to work with. You might want to try food from a specific region of the world. It's also really nice to use seasonal ingredients—also check any allergies of your guests.

3 MAKE A LIST

Create a big list of the ingredients and the amounts you need, then order the food so it arrives two days before.

4 MAKE IN ADVANCE

When it comes to food, it's all about the prep— make as much in advance as possible.

Starters

- Make-ahead starters like soup and dips are perfect.

Mains

- Roast veggies in advance which can be re-heated, and make sauces and dips etc the day before.
- One pot dishes like soups or curries are perfect for making ahead.
- Tray bakes are the perfect way of serving large groups. Tarts, cakes, pizzas, and roast vegetables work really well.
- I like to plate individual main dishes, then serve platters in the middle for guests to help themselves.

Desserts

- Choose a dessert which can be made and chilled the day before such as chocolate pots or cake. Then you can just dress and serve them on the day.
- Toppings like cashew cream can be made the day before and popped into piping bags which can be stored in the fridge, ready to be piped into pretty patterns.

5 SET THE SCENE

Have fun creating a fun theme—it could be anything from beach, historical or movie-themed, to a tea party. A centerpiece for your meal is helpful—this could be a big tart or even a baked squash. For your party to look like an abundant feast, make lots of smaller dishes.

INGREDIENTS

For the baked tofu

2 tbsp soy sauce

1 tbsp maple syrup

3 tbsp toasted sesame oil

1 tsp garlic powder

2 tbsp nutritional yeast

2 tbsp tomato purée

5 tbsp teriyaki sauce

½ tsp salt

1 block firm tofu

1 red pepper

½ cup mushrooms

1 zucchini

1 ½ cup sugar snaps

To serve

Noodles of choice

Handful of toasted salted peanuts

One-pan teriyaki tofu with veg & noodles

When it's cold outside, why not stay cozy at home instead of eating out or having takeout with my teriyaki tofu with veggies and noodles? This is such a simple, stress free and tasty recipe—it can be prepped ahead and then popped in the oven and cooked in minutes. The magic happens when the veggies and tofu bake in the glorious sauce.

TO MAKE THE TERIYAKI TOFU

1. Pre-heat your oven to 350°F.
2. Cut up the peppers, mushrooms, and zucchini.
3. Place the tofu in the middle of a medium roasting tray. Then place the veggies around the tofu.
4. Make the sauce by mixing all the ingredients in a jar.
5. Pour the sauce over the tofu and vegetables, ensuring that everything is coated.
6. Bake for 30 minutes.
7. Serve with noodles of your choice, topped with peanuts.

Niki's tip
Serve in bowls with noodles and crunchy peanuts or seeds.

INGREDIENTS
Serves 4–6

....

For the filling
1 large red onion

2 tbsp olive oil

4 cloves garlic

2 red peppers

¾ cup mushrooms

1⅓ cup cooked chestnuts

12 sundried tomatoes

½ cup walnuts

1 tbsp soy sauce

3 tbsp nutritional yeast

1 tbsp vegan Worcester sauce

¼ cup dried cranberries

1 tsp sea salt

Pinch of black pepper

For the pastry
2 x pre-made sheets dairy-free puff pastry

Plain flour, to dust

3 tbsp plant-based milk

1 tbsp English mustard

For the potatoes
1 kilo potatoes

2 tbsp olive oil

1 tsp sea salt

2 sprigs rosemary

Twist of black pepper

Mushroom & chestnut wellington with veggies

This is something special! Yes, it's a little bit more involved, but it's worth it for a celebratory meal with family or friends. I think my mushroom & chestnut wellington looks and tastes fantastic.

TO MAKE THE WELLINGTON
1. Finely chop the onion, garlic, peppers, and mushrooms.
2. Add the onion and oil to a medium pan and fry gently on a low heat for around 10 minutes until soft and browning.
3. Add the garlic and fry for a further minute. Next add the peppers and mushrooms and cook for 5–6 minutes until soft.
4. Chop up the sundried tomatoes, chestnuts, and walnuts roughly and add to the pan along with the remaining filling ingredients. Stir to combine.
5. Remove from the heat and leave to cool in the pan.
6. Line a large baking tray with baking paper.
7. In a small bowl, mix the milk and mustard together with a pinch of salt and set aside.
8. Unroll one of the puff pastry sheets onto the baking tray lined with baking parchment.
9. Now spoon the filling down the middle of the pastry sheet in a line, leaving a 2-inch border around the edges. Brush around the edge with the mustard milk mix.
10. Now carefully place the second pastry sheet over the top and press it down around the filling to remove any air.
11. Seal the edges by pressing with a fork to seal firmly, then trim off any excess pastry. Cut a steam hole in the top.
12. Re-roll the excess pastry and make leaf shapes if you like to place on top.
13. Pre-heat your oven to 350°F.

INGREDIENTS

....

For the peas and greens

1 onion

2 garlic cloves

16 oz frozen peas

8 oz greens of choice

Juice of 1 lemon

1 bunch mint, shredded

2 tbsp extra virgin olive oil

½ tsp sea salt

Pinch of black pepper

14. Brush with the remaining milk mix over the top of the wellington and place in the oven.

15. Bake for 35–40 minutes until puffed up and crispy.

16. Cut into slices to serve.

TO ROAST THE POTATOES

1. Pre-heat your oven to 350°F.

2. Add the potatoes to a roasting tray then toss to coat them in olive oil, rosemary, salt, and pepper.

3. Roast for about 40 minutes until crispy on the outside and soft inside.

TO MAKE THE PEAS & GREENS

1. Firstly chop the onion and slice the garlic.

2. Add the onions and oil to a pan and fry on medium until soft around 8–10 minutes. Add the garlic and fry for a further minute.

3. Now add all the remaining ingredients and cook for 2–3 minutes until the greens have wilted.

Making festive
PRESENTS

There's no better way to show your friends and family that you love them than through food. Why not make a home-made gift to show your love and make someone's day? You can make it in advance and send your special present in lovely packaging to make it even more special. Here are some ideas!

CHOCOLATES & TRUFFLES

There's just something so decadent and special about a truffle or homemade chocolate, and they're much easier to make than you think.

TURN PAGE for my pretty chocolate mendiants recipe.

CHOCOLATE BARK

You can choose the toppings they love the most, from chopped fruits and nuts, to pretzels and candy or even broken up chocolate bars! It's also a great way to use up any leftover ingredients that you don't have enough of to make something out of—just mix it all together and throw it on top!

COOKIES

These are always a great choice, as they stay fresh for a few days if you keep them in an air-tight container, and you can completely customize them. You can add chopped nuts or fruits or decorate with icing and sprinkles—go crazy, let your creativity go wild!

CARAMELIZED NUTS

I love making deliciously sticky caramelized nuts—you can add whatever sweet spices you have on hand. My favorites include cinnamon, vanilla, allspice, nutmeg, a touch of clove powder, and a dash of salt for balance.

MUFFINS OR CUPCAKES

Everyone loves cupcakes and muffins, don't they? A little individual cake made just for you! Choose festive flavors like warming spices, gingerbread, and of course chocolate. Cupcakes are super portable—make the toppings and packaging pretty and personalized.

JAM/CHUTNEY

The ultimate make ahead present—turn your glut of summer produce into your own jam or chutney. Add some festive spices like cloves and allspice to make them extra special.

TURN TO PAGE 79 for my jam and chutney recipes.

Chocolate mendiants

These cute and delicious little chocolate mendiants are so easy to make and make lovely edible gifts. Top them with anything you like—pistachios and cranberries look particularly festive with their contrasting colors.

INGREDIENTS
Makes approx. 30

....

7.5 oz dairy-free dark chocolate

Toppings
Pistachios
Mixed fruit peel
Chopped nuts
Cranberries

TO MAKE THE CHOCOLATE MENDIANTS

1. Boil a kettle of water, then pour into a medium saucepan.
2. Place a glass bowl over the top (make sure it doesn't touch the water).
3. Break up the chocolate into small pieces and add them to the bowl.
4. Simmer until the chocolate has melted—don't stir it. Remove from the heat.
5. Line a large baking tray with baking paper then spoon small amounts of melted chocolate on to the paper.
6. Spread out to form small circles.
7. Sprinkle your toppings of choice on top.
8. Set aside to cool completely and firm up.
9. When set you can store in the fridge.

Niki's tip
Other delicious toppings include vegan marshmallows or whole nuts. Edible flowers are super pretty too!

Spiced clementine fizz

A little bit of festive fizz! Sweet clementine juice with lovely bubbly ginger beer and lots of mint and ice seems like a wonderful celebration drink to me. This also works well with blood oranges when they're in season.

INGREDIENTS
Serves 2

....

Juice of 2 clementines

2 tsp vegan sugar

1 tsp vanilla extract

A few drops of orange blossom water or orange extract

Handful of mint

2 cups ginger beer

Lots of ice

TO MAKE THE SPICED CLEMENTINE FIZZ

1. Juice the clementines and add to a jar along with the sugar, vanilla, and orange blossom water. Stir to combine.
2. Pour into two glasses then top up with ice.
3. Pour in the ginger beer and stir in the fresh mint.

INGREDIENTS
Makes approx. 8

For the onion bhajis
2 large red onions
1 ¼ cup gram flour
1 tsp garam masala
1 tsp ground cumin
1 tsp cilantro
1 tsp garlic powder
1 tsp ground turmeric
Pinch chili flakes
1 tsp salt
6 oz water
Handful fresh cilantro
4 tbsp vegetable oil

Onion bhajis & cheat's samosas

These tasty Indian-themed treats are the perfect snack—lightly spiced and entirely addictive. The bhajis are really easy to make and are fantastic for dipping in some mango chutney or mint dip. The samosas are actually very easy to make, so don't be scared of the list of instructions. Make sure you eat them right away while they're super crispy!

TO MAKE THE ONION BHAJIS

1. Peel and slice the onions into thin rings.
2. In a large bowl add all dry ingredients, mix, then add the water and cilantro.
3. Stir to form a thick batter.
4. Now add the onions and mix well to coat.
5. Allow to sit for 15 minutes so the onions soften.
6. Add the vegetable oil into a large non-stick frying pan so there is a shallow layer of oil.
7. Heat the oil to medium/high then spoon 2 tablespoons of the mix into the pan. Repeat twice more, then press each one down a bit.
8. Fry for 4–5 minutes until crispy and golden. Flip and repeat.
9. Continue until you have used up all the mix.
10. Place on a plate lined with paper towels to remove any excess oil.

INGREDIENTS
Makes 8

For the samosa filling

1 red onion

1 tbsp vegetable oil

4 garlic cloves

2 tsp cumin seeds

1 tsp turmeric

1 tsp black mustard seeds

1 tsp garam masala

2 medium tomatoes

1 ½ cup frozen peas

Juice of ½ a lemon

Handful of fresh cilantro & mint

½ tsp salt

Pinch of chili flakes

For the pastry

½ pack of vegan filo pastry sheets

Sesame seeds for topping

To serve

Mango chutney

TO MAKE THE CHEAT'S SAMOSA FILLING

1. Peel and dice the onion.
2. Add the oil to a frying pan over a medium heat, add the onion, and fry for 8 minutes.
3. Now add the garlic and spices and stir to combine and fry for a further minute.
4. Chop up the tomatoes and add them to the pan and fry for 5 minutes until softened.
5. Stir in the frozen peas and remaining ingredients, and cook for 2–3 minutes.

TO ROLL

1. Unroll the filo pastry.
2. Slice the sheets in half lengthwise, then select one to fill.
3. Brush your sheet with oil, then spoon 2 tbsp of the mix into a bottom corner to create a triangle.
4. Next fold the pastry over the mix to create a triangle, then repeat this fold until you've run out of pastry and have an inch or so left.
5. Finally, tuck the pastry into the samosa.
6. Repeat until you've used up all the mixture and assembled 8 samosas.

TO COOK

1. Pre-heat your oven to 350°F.
2. Pop the samosas onto a baking tray, brush with a little oil, then sprinkle one side with sesame seeds.
3. Bake for 25–30 minutes until the filo is golden brown and crispy.
4. Serve with mango chutney.

INGREDIENTS

1 tbsp olive oil
1 red onion
2 garlic cloves
1 tsp cumin seeds
2 tsp smoked paprika
½ teaspoon caraway seeds
2 tomatoes
2 cups veggie mince
2 tbsp soy sauce
3 tbsp sun dried tomato paste
1 tsp salt
Pinch of chili flakes

For the hummus

1 ½ cups cooked chickpeas
Juice of ½ a lemon
1 clove garlic
2 tbsp olive oil
1 tsp harissa paste
1 tbsp tahini
1 tbsp sundried tomato puree
Salt to taste

Toppings

Pita/bread
Shredded mint
Plant based yogurt

Harissa dip party platter

There's nothing I love more than a big layered party platter ready for dipping into. This one has a base of harissa hummus, topped with spiced veggie mince. It takes its inspiration from Lebanese kawarma (hummus topped with lamb) and it's delicious. All the warming spices make it a perfect seasonal dish. It's best served with fresh bread or crudités—yum!

TO MAKE THE VEGGIE TOPPING

1. Chop the onion and garlic.
2. Now add the onion and oil to a frying pan and fry on a medium heat for 8–9 minutes until soft.
3. Now add the garlic and spices and stir to combine.
4. Add the mince, tomato puree, tomatoes, and soy and fry for 12–15 minutes until the mince is cooked through.
5. Now add a pinch of chili flakes and a pinch of salt. Stir to combine.

TO MAKE THE HUMMUS

1. Add all the ingredients to a food processor and blend until very smooth and creamy.
2. Top the hummus with the veggie topping, fresh mint, and yogurt.

Niki's tip

The key to super creamy hummus is blending for at least 2–3 minutes in your food processor.

Peanut butter pecan pie

This is a special dessert—a crunchy, chocolatey base with the dreamiest of creamy fillings. There's no cooking involved—just a matter of blending and putting in the fridge to firm up. The secret ingredient which makes the filling so creamy is silken tofu, which sounds strange but it makes the most amazing smooth chocolate mousse. This is most definitely worthy of any party or festive table!

INGREDIENTS

For the crust
3.5 oz pecans
3.5 oz ground almonds
2 tbsp peanut butter
2 tbsp cacao powder
2 tbsp maple syrup
3 medjool dates pitted
Pinch salt

For the filling
5 medjool dates, pitted
2 tbsp peanut butter
1 tsp almond extract
1 tsp vanilla extract
1 tbsp coconut oil
Pinch sea salt flakes
12 oz soft silken tofu
2 tbsp cacao powder
2 tbsp maple syrup

Toppings
1 ¾ cup pecans
2 tbsp maple syrup
Sea salt flakes

TO MAKE THE PECAN PIE

1. Grease a 10-inch loose bottom pie tin.
2. To make the crust, add the pecans to your food processor or high-speed blender and blend until crumbly.
3. Add in the rest of the crust ingredients, and blend again until everything comes together.
4. With your hands, press the mixture onto the bottom and sides of your pie tin.
5. Wash out your mixer and add in the filling ingredients. Blend until smooth and creamy—it will be a few minutes before all the dates are thoroughly blended in.
6. Dollop the filling onto the base and smooth it out.
7. To toast the nuts, add the pecans to a small pan and heat to medium. Dry toast until the pecans are a little toasted.
8. Turn off the heat and tip into a bowl. Now add the maple syrup and sea salt. Stir to combine.
9. When the nuts have cooled down, top the tart with the toasted nuts.
10. Transfer to the fridge for at least 1 hour to firm up. Store in the fridge until it's time to eat.

INGREDIENTS
Serves 8–12

....

6 oz dark dairy-free chocolate, broken up

3 tbsp vegetable oil

4 oz ground almonds

4 tbsp white self-rising flour

½ cup light brown vegan sugar

4 tbsp cacao powder

2 tsp baking powder

1 tsp vanilla extract

3 tbsp plant-based yogurt

Pinch sea salt

1 cup plant-based milk

For the ganache
4 oz dark dairy-free chocolate, broken up

1.5 oz vegan butter

1 tbsp maple syrup

Toppings
Pistachios, crushed

Rich chocolate & almond cake

If you are partial to a rich chocolate dessert, you'll love this. It's a soft and dense cake topped with chocolate ganache and pistachios, which makes the cake look very glamorous.

TO MAKE THE CAKE
1. Pre-heat your oven to 350°F.
2. Prepare a loose-bottomed cake tin by greasing and lining it with baking paper.
3. Add the chocolate and oil to a saucepan and heat on a very low heat, stirring occasionally until the chocolate has melted.
4. Now add all the ingredients along with the melted chocolate to a food processor and blend until you get a thick batter.
5. Spoon into the tin and bake on a medium heat for 30–35 minutes or until cooked through.
6. Allow to cool then remove from the cake tin.

TO MAKE THE TOPPING
1. Add the chocolate, butter, and maple syrup to a glass bowl and microwave for around 30 seconds until melted, then gently mix.
2. Allow to cool a little then spoon onto the top of the cake and spread to the edges.
3. Sprinkle with the crushed pistachios and pop in the fridge to firm up.
4. Store in the fridge.

Frequently asked QUESTIONS

Q. You can't be 100% vegan, can you?

A. Well, probably not—as animals or animal derivatives are used in manufacturing processes, and it's almost impossible to check the label on everything you consume (plus sometimes it's hard to understand the terminology). But you can make a conscious choice to adopt a vegan diet and make ethical purchase decisions.

Q. Veganism is just a fad, right?

A. No way! These days, so many people are making lifestyle choices based on minimizing the harm to the world, animals, and their own bodies. It's hard to imagine that this will diminish in the coming years.

Q. Why should I eat seasonally?

A. Reasons it's great to eat seasonally include:
- It tastes better and it's fresher.
- You're helping the environment, because buying local or seasonal produce means less food miles. Food production and transport release greenhouse gases like carbon dioxide and fossil fuels, which contribute to acid rain, air pollution, and global warming. Eating seasonally and locally can help cut down on environmental impact.
- You can support local small businesses and farmers.
- Eating in season saves you money as prices usually go down on seasonal produce as there are less shipping and storing costs.
- It's an opportunity to be creative!

Q. How can I celebrate with my friends if I'm vegan?

A. You shouldn't worry about that at all. There are now plenty of pre-made options in the shops and you can find lots of delicious things to make within these pages to impress your friends and family.

Q. **Will I need lots of tools to grow my own food?**

A. It's best to start small, experiment, and take it from there. If it's something you love, you can invest in some tools to start growing more seriously.

Q. **Will I be lacking in protein? Especially if I do a lot of exercise...**

A. It's very unlikely you'll be lacking in protein—there are many easy ways to incorporate plant-based protein into your meals.

Q. **Will I get enough B12?**

A. You'll definitely need a source of vitamin B12, so lots of products are now fortified with B12 including non-organic plant milks, breakfast cereals, and nutritional yeast. If you're worried, a supplement may be an option.

Q. **Aren't you going to be deficient in vitamins & minerals if you don't eat meat?**

A. You can get what you need from a balanced plant-based diet, as most of the key nutrients are also found in plants.

Q. **Do vegans only eat rabbit food?**

A. No chance! The range of vegan food has never been wider, and it's growing every day—plus you'll find a huge variety of ingredients in the recipes in this book.

Q. **What is nutritional yeast—is it the same as baking yeast?**

A. Nutritional yeast is different—it's de-activated yeast. It has a nutty, cheesy, savory flavor and is used as a vegan cheese substitute. You can find it in health food shops—it's a game changer.

Q. **Is soy bad for the environment?**

A. Soy is a fantastic source of plant-based protein but is also a main cause of rainforest deforestation. However, 70% of the world's soy is fed directly to livestock, and only 6% is turned into human food.

Glossary

USEFUL TERMS

CRUELTY-FREE
Not tested on animals.

DAIRY-FREE
Contains no dairy products like cow's milk, cheese, butter, yogurt, or cream.

ETHICAL VEGANISM
Ethical vegans are those who don't just eat a plant-based diet, but also oppose the use of animals in any part of their life, including clothing, animal testing, and animal labor.

FLEXITARIANISM
A flexitarian is someone who still eats meat and dairy, but is trying to include more plant-based meals in their diet.

PESCETARIANISM
Vegetarians who also eat seafood are known as pescetarians.

PLANT-BASED
A plant-based diet consists of plants including vegetables, fruit, pulses, grains, nuts, and seeds. Not necessarily the same as vegan, as some plant products can cause cruelty to animals, and "plant-based" usually only relates to food, not wider vegan concerns.

VEGANISM
According to the Vegan Society, "a way of living which seeks to exclude, as far as is possible and practicable, all forms of exploitation of, and cruelty to, animals for food, clothing, or any other purpose."

VEGETARIANISM
The practice of avoiding any meat products, including red meat, poultry, and seafood. Most vegetarians still eat eggs and dairy products like cow's milk and cheese.

COOKING TECHNIQUES AND INGREDIENTS

Baking powder – A dry leavening agent, used to increase the volume and lighten the texture of baked goods.

Baking soda – A mixture of sodium and hydrogen carbonate. When it's mixed with an acid (such as vinegar) it creates carbon dioxide which causes the mixture to expand before it's replaced with air.

Beat – To mix vigorously with a spoon, mixer, or spatula

Blend – To make a liquid using a food processor or blender.

Boil – To heat liquid until it bubbles.

Chop – To cut something into small pieces.

Combine – To mix ingredients together.

Dice – To cut into small cubes.

Dissolve – To melt or liquify something, usually into water.

Drain – To remove excess liquid, using a sieve or colander.

Drizzle – To pour slowly.

Fold – To fold something into a batter without stirring, i.e. choc chips into cake batter.

Grate – To shred into small pieces using a grater.

Grease – To rub oil or spread onto a baking tray or tin to stop sticking.

Harissa – Hot sauce or paste made from chili pepper, paprika, and oil.

Knead – To fold and squash dough repeatedly, to make it more elastic.

Juice – To squeeze liquid out.

Lukewarm – Mildly warm, not hot.

Mince – To chop into very small pieces.

Pre-heat – To turn on the oven so it can reach the correct temperature before cooking or baking.

Pulse – Any food from the legume family, including peas, beans, chickpeas, soybeans, and lentils.

Purée – To blend fruit or vegetables to a thick pulp.

Rinse – To clean by washing under cold water.

Season – To add salt and pepper to dishes to add flavor.

Sauté – To cook/fry in a pan with oil.

Seitan – Wheat gluten, used to make meat substitutes.

Set – To leave food until it firms up.

Simmer – To heat liquid in a pan on a low heat, until small bubbles rise from it.

Soy – A legume native to east Asia. The bean is used to make soy milk, tofu, soy sauce, and tempeh.

Stir fry – To fry rapidly over a high heat, stirring constantly to prevent burning.

Tempeh – A soybean curd, chewier and denser than tofu.

Tofu – A curd made of processed soybeans.

Tahini – Sesame seed paste.

Whip – To beat something to incorporate more air into it.

Whisk – To mix vigorously with a whisk.

Zest – The grated skin of any citrus fruit.

Index

Notes